booties , blankets and bears

booties, blankets and bears

20 irresistible hand knits for your baby

Debbie Bliss

photography by Ulla Nyeman

T
TRAFALGAR SQUARE
North Pomfret, Vermont

knitting basics 8

patterns 36

in a box of **booties**

knitting basics

types of yarns

When choosing a yarn for children's hand knits, it is important that you work with a fiber that is soft but also practical. Children are often more used to the lightweight freedom of fleeces, and they can be resistant to hand knits that they may consider scratchy and uncomfortable.

The yarns I have chosen for the designs in this book are either an extra fine merino or cashmere mixes. Although they create fabrics that are gentle against the skin, the other essential feature is that they are machine washable.

When knitting a garment, always make the effort to buy the yarn specified in the pattern. All these designs have been created with a specific yarn in mind. A different yarn may not produce the same quality of fabric or have the same wash and wear properties. From an aesthetic point of view, the clarity of a subtle stitch pattern may be lost if a garment is knitted in an inferior yarn.

However, there may be occasions when a knitter needs to substitute a yarn—if the wearer has an allergy to wool, for example—and so the following is a guide to making the most informed choices.

Always buy a yarn that is the same weight as the one given in the pattern—replace a double knitting with a double knitting, for example—and check that the recommended gauge of both yarns is the same.

Where you are substituting a different fiber, be aware of the design.

A cable pattern knitted in cotton when worked in wool will pull in because of the greater elasticity of the yarn and so the fabric will become narrower; this will alter the proportions of the garment.

Check the yardage of the yarn. Yarns that weigh the same may have different lengths in the ball or hank, so you may need to buy more or less yarn.

Here are descriptions of my yarns and a guide to their weights and types:

Debbie Bliss Baby Cashmerino:
A fine-weight yarn between a UK "4-ply" and a double knitting.
55% merino wool, 33% microfiber, 12% cashmere.
Approximately 137yd/50g ball.
Debbie Bliss Cashmerino Aran:
55% merino wool, 33% microfiber, 12% cashmere.
Approximately 99yd/50g ball.
Debbie Bliss Cashmerino Double Knitting: 55% merino wool, 33% microfiber, 12% cashmere.
Approximately 120yd/50g ball.
Debbie Bliss Rialto Double Knitting:
100% merino wool extra fine superwash.
Approximately 115yd/50g ball.

Debbie Bliss Rialto Aran:
100% merino wool extra fine superwash.
Approximately 87yd/50g ball.

buying yarn
The yarn label will carry all the essential information you need as to gauge, needle size, weight, and yardage. Importantly, it will also have a dye lot number. Yarns are dyed in batches or lots, which can vary considerably. As your yarn store may not have the same dye lot later on, buy all your yarn for a project at the same time. If you know that sometimes you use more yarn than that quoted in a pattern, buy extra. If it is not possible to buy all the yarn you need with the same dye lot number, use the different ones where the shade change will not show as much, on a neck or border, as a change of dye lot across a main piece will be more obvious.

It is also a good idea at the time of buying the yarn to check the pattern and make sure that you already have the needles you will require. If not, buy them now because it will save a lot of frustration when you get home.

garment care

Taking care of your hand knits is important because you want them to look good for as long as possible. Correct washing is particularly important for children's garments as they need to be washed often.

Check the yarn label for washing instructions to see whether the yarn is hand or machine washable, and if it is the latter, at what temperature it should be washed.

Most hand knits should be dried flat on an absorbent cloth, such as a towel, to soak up any moisture. Laying them flat in this way gives you an opportunity to pat the garment back into shape if it has become pulled around in the washing machine. Even if you are in a hurry, do not be tempted to dry your knits near a direct heat source, such as a radiator.

As children's garments are small, you may prefer to hand wash them. Use a washing agent that is specifically designed for knitwear since this will be kinder to the fabric. Use warm rather than hot water, and handle the garment gently without rubbing or wringing. Let the water out of the sink and then gently squeeze out the excess water. Do not lift out a water-logged knit as the weight of the water will pull it out of shape. You may need to remove more moisture by rolling it in a towel. Dry flat as explained before.

techniques

cast on

Your first step when beginning to knit is to work a foundation row called a cast-on. Without this row you cannot begin to knit.

There are several methods of casting on. You can choose a method to serve a particular purpose or because you feel comfortable with that technique. The two cast-ons on pages 16 and 17 are the ones I have found to be the most popular—the thumb and the cable methods.

In order to work a cast-on edge, you must first make a slip knot.

slip knot

1 Wind the yarn around the fingers on your left hand to make a circle of yarn as shown above. With the knitting needle, pull a loop of the yarn attached to the ball through the yarn circle on your fingers.

2 Pull both ends of the yarn to tighten the slip knot on the knitting needle. You are now ready to begin, using either of the following cast-on techniques.

cast on

thumb cast-on

1 Make a slip knot as shown on page 15, leaving a long tail. With the slip knot on the needle in your right hand and the yarn that comes from the ball over your index finger, wrap the tail end of the yarn over your left thumb from front to back, holding the yarn in your palm with your fingers.

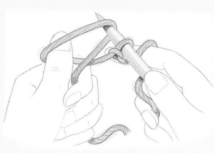

2 Insert the knitting needle upward through the yarn loop on your left thumb.

The thumb cast-on is a one-needle method that produces a flexible edge, which makes it particularly useful for nonelastic yarns such as cotton. The "give" in it also makes it a good cast-on to use where the edge will turn back, as on the booties with the blanket stitch detail (see page 56).

Unlike with two-needle methods, you are working toward the yarn end, which means you have to predict the length you need to cast on the required number of stitches. Otherwise you may find you do not have enough yarn to complete the last few stitches and have to start all over again. If unsure, always allow for more yarn than you think you need as you can use what is left over for sewing seams.

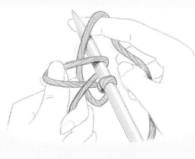

3 With the right index finger, wrap the yarn from the ball up and over the tip of the knitting needle.

4 Draw the yarn through the loop on your thumb to form a new stitch on the knitting needle. Then, let the yarn loop slip off your left thumb and pull the loose end to tighten up the stitch. Repeat these steps until the required number of stitches have been cast on.

cable cast-on

1 Make a slip knot as shown on page 15. Hold the knitting needle with the slip knot in your left hand and insert the right-hand needle from left to right and from front to back through the slip knot. Wrap the yarn from the ball up and over the tip of the right-hand needle as shown.

2 With the right-hand needle, draw a loop through the slip knot to make a new stitch. Do not drop the stitch from the left-hand needle, but instead slip the new stitch onto the left-hand needle as shown.

The cable cast-on method uses two needles and is particularly good for ribbed edges, as it provides a sturdy, but still elastic, edge. As you need to insert the needle between the stitches and pull the yarn through to create another stitch make sure that you do not make the new stitch too tight. The cable method is one of the most widely used cast-ons.

3 Next, insert the right-hand needle between the two stitches on the left-hand needle and wrap the yarn around the tip of the right-hand needle.

4 Pull the yarn through to make a new stitch, and then place the new stitch on the left-hand needle as before. Repeat the last two steps until the required number of stitches have been cast on.

knit & purl

The knit and purl stitches form the basis of almost all knitted fabrics. The knit stitch is the easiest to learn and is the first stitch you will create. When worked continuously it forms a reversible fabric called garter stitch. You can recognize garter stitch by the horizontal ridges formed at the top of the knitted loops.

After the knit stitch you will move on to the purl stitch. If the purl stitch is worked continuously, it forms the same fabric as garter stitch. However, if purl and knit rows are worked alternately, they create stockinette stitch, which is the most widely used knitted fabric.

knit

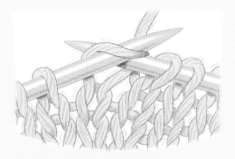

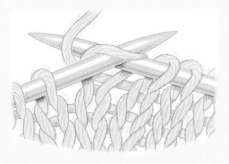

1 With the cast-on stitches on the needle in your left hand, insert the right-hand needle from left to right and from front to back through the first cast-on stitch.

2 Take the yarn from the ball on your index finger (the working yarn) around the tip of the right-hand needle.

3 Draw the right-hand needle and yarn through the stitch, thus forming a new stitch on the right-hand needle, and at the same time slip the original stitch off the left-hand needle. Repeat these steps until all the stitches from the left-hand needle have been worked. One knit row has now been completed.

purl

1 With the yarn at the front of the work, insert the right-hand needle from the right to the left into the front of the first stitch on the left-hand needle.

2 Then take the yarn from the ball on your index finger (the working yarn) around the tip of the right-hand needle.

3 Draw the right-hand needle and the yarn through the stitch, thus forming a new stitch on the right-hand needle, and at the same time slip the original stitch off the left-hand needle. Repeat these steps until all the stitches have been worked. One purl row has now been completed.

increase

Increases are used to add to the width of the knitted fabric by creating more stitches. They are worked, for example, when shaping sleeves up the length of the arm or when additional stitches are needed after a ribbed border. Some increases are invisible, while others are worked away from the edge of the work and are meant to be seen in order to provide decorative detail. Most knitting patterns will tell you which type of increase to make.

increase one ("kfb")

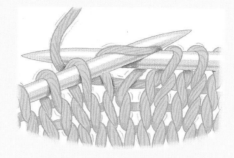

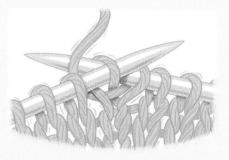

1 Insert the right-hand needle into the front of the next stitch, then knit the stitch but leave it on the left-hand needle.

2 Insert the right-hand needle into the back of the same stitch and knit it. Then slip the original stitch off the needle. Now you have made an extra stitch on the right-hand needle.

make one ("m1")

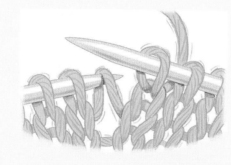

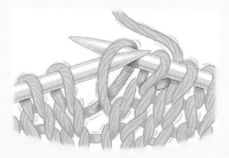

1 Insert the left-hand needle from front to back under the horizontal strand between the stitch just worked on the right-hand needle and the first stitch on the left-hand needle.

2 Knit into the back of the loop to twist it, and to prevent a hole. Drop the strand from the left-hand needle. This forms a new stitch on the right-hand needle.

yarn over ("yo")

yarn over between knit stitches
Bring the yarn forward between
the two needles, from the back to
the front of the work. Taking the
yarn over the right-hand needle
to do so, knit the next stitch.

yarn over between purl stitches
Take the yarn over the right-hand
needle to the back, then between the
two needles to the front. Then purl
the next stitch.

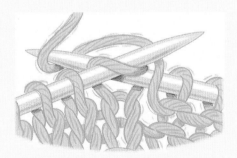

yarn over between a purl and a knit
Take the yarn from the front over
the right-hand needle to the back.
Then knit the next stitch.

yarn over between a knit and a purl
Bring the yarn forward between the
two needles from the back to the front
of the work, and take it over the top
of the right-hand needle to the back
again and then forward between the
needles. Then purl the next stitch.

bind off

knit bind-off

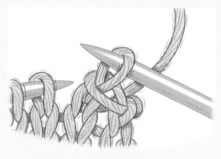

1 Knit two stitches. Insert the left-hand needle into the first stitch knitted on the right-hand needle and lift this stitch over the second stitch and off the right-hand needle.

2 One stitch is now on the right-hand needle. Knit the next stitch. Repeat the first step until all the stitches have been bound off. Pull the yarn through the last stitch to fasten off.

purl bind-off

Binding off is used to finish off your knitted piece so that the stitches don't unravel. It is also used to decrease more than one stitch at a time, such as when shaping armholes, neckbands, and buttonholes. It is important that a bind-off is firm but elastic, particularly when you are binding off around a neckband, to ensure that it can be pulled easily over the head. Unless told otherwise, bind off in the stitch pattern used in the piece.

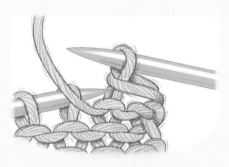

1 Purl two stitches. Insert the left-hand needle into the front of the first stitch worked on the right-hand needle and lift this stitch over the second stitch and off the right-hand needle.

2 One stitch is now on the right-hand needle. Purl the next stitch. Repeat the first step until all the stitches have been bound off. Pull the yarn through the last stitch to fasten off.

decrease

knit 2 together

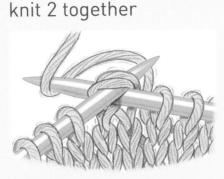

knit 2 together ("k2tog" or "dec one")
On a knit row, insert the right-hand needle from left to right through the next two stitches on the left-hand needle and knit them together. One stitch has been decreased.

purl 2 together

purl 2 together ("p2tog" or "dec one")
On a purl row, insert the right-hand needle from right to left through the next two stitches on the left-hand needle. Then purl them together. One stitch has been decreased.

Decreases are used to make the fabric narrower by getting rid of stitches on the needle. They are worked to make an opening for a neckline or shaping a sleeve cap. As with increases, they can be used to create decorative detail, often around a neck edge. Increases and decreases are used together to create lace patterns.

slip stitch over

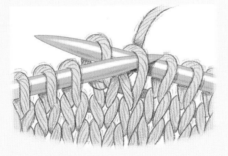

slip 1, knit 1, pass slipped stitch over ("psso")
1 Insert the right-hand needle into the next stitch on the left-hand needle and slip it onto the right-hand needle without knitting it. Knit the next stitch. Then insert the left-hand needle into the slipped stitch as shown.

2 With the left-hand needle, lift the slipped stitch over the knitted stitch as shown and off the right-hand needle.

reading patterns

To those unfamiliar with knitting patterns they can appear to be written in a strange, alien language! However, as you become used to the terminology you will see that they have a logic and consistency that you will soon become familiar with.

Do not be too concerned if you read through a pattern first and are confused by parts of it because some instructions make more sense when your stitches are on the needle and you are at that point in the piece. However, it is sometimes a good idea to check with your yarn store whether your skill levels are up to a particular design to prevent frustration later on.

Figures for larger sizes are given in parentheses ( ). Where only one figure appears, it means that this number applies to all sizes. Directions in brackets [ ] should be repeated as many times as instructed. Where 0 (zero) appears, no stitches or rows are worked for this size.

When you follow the pattern, it is important that you consistently use the right stitches or rows for your size. Switching between sizes can be avoided by marking your size throughout with a highlighting pen on a photocopy of the pattern.

Before starting your project, check the size and the actual measurements that are quoted for that size, you may want to make a smaller or larger garment depending on the proportions of the wearer it is intended for.

The quantities of yarn given in the instructions are based on the yarn used by the knitter of the original garment, therefore all amounts should be considered approximate. For example, if that knitter has used almost all of the last ball, it may be that another knitter with a slightly different gauge has to start another ball to complete the garment. A slight variation in gauge can therefore make the difference between using fewer or more balls than stated in the pattern.

gauge

Every knitting pattern gives a gauge— the number of stitches and rows to 4 inches that should be obtained with the specified yarn, needle size, and stitch pattern. It is essential to check your gauge before starting your project. A slight variation can alter the proportions of the finished garment and the look of the fabric. A gauge that is too loose will produce an uneven and unstable fabric that can drop or lose its shape after washing, while one that is too tight can make a hard, inelastic fabric.

Making a gauge square
Use the same needles, yarn, and stitch pattern quoted in the gauge note in the pattern. Knit a sample at last 5 inches square to get the most accurate result. Smooth out the finished sample on a flat surface, making sure you are not

stretching it out. To check the stitch gauge, place a tape measure or ruler horizontally on the sample and mark 4 inches with pins (see below). Count the number of stitches between the pins. To check the row gauge, mark 4 inches with pins vertically and count the number of rows. If the number of stitches and rows is greater than specified in the pattern, your gauge is tighter and you should change to a larger needle and make another gauge square. If there are fewer stitches and rows, your gauge is looser and you should try again on a smaller needle size.

The stitch gauge is the most important to get right, since the number of stitches in a pattern are set. The length, however, is often given as a measurement rather than in rows, and you may be able to simply work more or fewer rows.

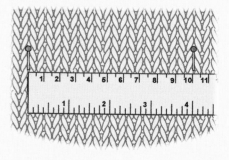

abbreviations

The following are the general abbreviation used throughout this book. If any special abbreviations are needed, they are provided at the beginning of the individual patterns.

standard abbreviations

alt = alternate

beg = begin(ning)

cont = continu(e)(ing)

dec = decreas(e)(ing)

foll = follow(s)(ing)

g = gram(s)

garter st = garter stitch (k every row)

in = inch(es)

inc = increase(e)(ing)

k = knit

kfb = knit into front and back of next st

M1 = make one stitch by picking up the loop lying between the stitch just worked and the next stitch and working into the back of it

mm = millimeter(s)

patt = pattern; or work in pattern

p = purl

psso = pass slipped stitch over

rem = remain(s)(ing)

rep = repeat(s)(ing)

skp = slip 1, knit 1, pass slipped stitch over

sl = slip

ssk = [slip 1 knitwise] twice, insert tip of left-hand needle from left to right through slipped sts and k2tog

st(s) = stitch(es)

St st = stockinette stitch

tbl = through back of loop(s)

tog = together

yd = yard(s)

yo = yarn over right-hand needle to make a new stitch (see page 21)

cables

back cross 6-stitch cable ("C6B")

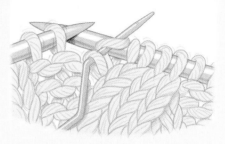

1 Slip the first three cable stitches purlwise off the left-hand needle and onto the cable needle. Leave the cable needle at the back of the work, then knit the next three stitches on the left-hand needle, keeping the yarn tight to prevent a gap from forming in the knitting.

2 Knit the three stitches directly from the cable needle, or if preferred, slip the three stitches from the cable needle back onto the left-hand needle and then knit them. This completes the cable cross.

front cross 6-stitch cable ("C6F")

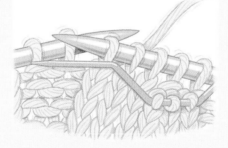

1 Slip the first three cable stitches purlwise off the left-hand needle and onto the cable needle. Leave the cable needle at the front of the work, then knit the next three stitches on the left-hand needle, keeping the yarn tight to prevent a gap from forming in the knitting.

2 Knit the three stitches directly from the cable needle, or if preferred, slip the three stitches from the cable needle back onto the left-hand needle and then knit them. This completes the cable cross.

Cables are formed by the simple technique of crossing one set of stitches over another. Stitches are held on a cable needle (a short double-pointed needle) at the back or front of the work while the same amount of stitches is worked from the left-hand needle. Simple cables form a vertical twisted rope of stockinette stitch on a background of reverse stockinette stitch and are most frequently worked over four or six stitches.

intarsia

Intarsia is used when you are working with larger areas of usually isolated color, such as when knitting large motifs. If the yarn not in use were stranded or woven into the wrong side, it could show through to the front or pull in the colorwork. In intarsia you use a separate strand or small ball of yarn for each color area and then twist colors together where they meet to prevent a gap from forming.

vertical

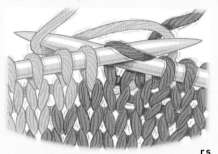

rs

ws

right diagonal

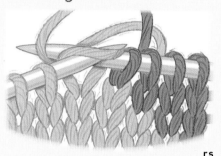

rs

ws

left diagonal

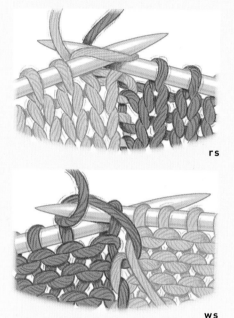

rs

ws

changing colors on a vertical line
If the two color areas are forming a vertical line, to change colors on a knit row drop the color you were using. Pick up the new color and wrap it around the dropped color as shown, then continue with the new color. Twist the yarns together on knit and purl rows in this same way at vertical-line color changes.

changing colors on a right diagonal
If the two color areas are forming a right diagonal line, on a knit row drop the color you were using. Pick up the new color and wrap it around the dropped color as shown, then continue with the new color. Twist the yarns together on knit rows only at right-diagonal color changes.

changing colors on a left diagonal
If the two color areas are forming a left diagonal line, on a purl row drop the color you were using. Pick up the new color and wrap it around the color just dropped as shown, then continue with the new color. Twist the yarns together on purl rows only at left-diagonal color changes.

reading charts

Most color patterns are worked from a chart rather than set out in the text. Each square represents a stitch and row, and the symbol or color within it will tell you which color to use. There will be a key listing the symbols used and the color they represent.

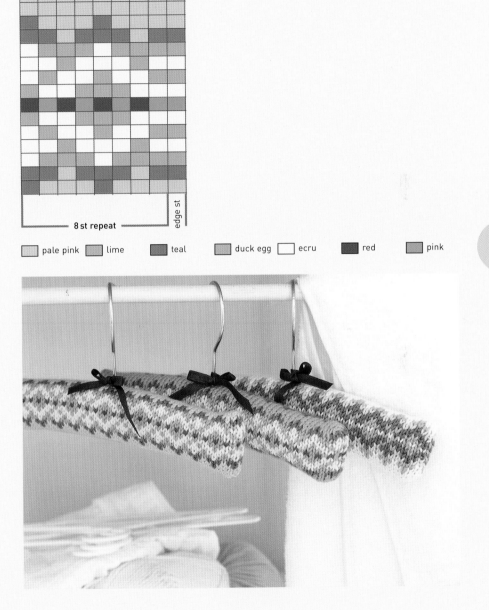

8 st repeat   edge st

pale pink   lime   teal   duck egg   ecru   red   pink

Unless stated otherwise, the first row of the chart is worked from right to left and represents the first right-side row of your knitting. The second chart row represents the second row (a wrong-side row) and is read and worked from left to right.

If the color pattern is a repeated design, as in Fair Isle, the chart will tell you how many stitches are in each repeat. You will repeat these stitches as many times as is required. At each side of the repeat there may be edge stitches—these are only worked at the beginning and end of the rows and they indicate where you need to start and end for the piece you are knitting. Most color patterns are worked in stockinette stitch.

stranding

stranding on a knit row

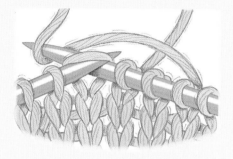 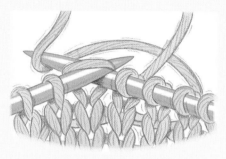

1 On a right-side (knit) row, to change colors drop the color you were using. Pick up the new color, take it over the top of the dropped color and start knitting with it.

2 To change back to the old color, drop the color you were knitting with. Pick up the old color, take it under the dropped color and knit to the next color change, and so on.

stranding on a purl row

1 On a wrong-side (purl) row, to change colors drop the color you were using. Pick up the new color, take it over the top of the dropped color and start purling with it.

2 To change back to the old color, drop the color you were knitting with. Pick up the old color, take it under the dropped color and purl to the next color change, and so on.

Stranding is used when each of two colors is worked over a small number of stitches. The color you are not using is left hanging on the wrong side of the work and is then picked up when it is needed again. This creates strands at the back of the work called floats. Care must be taken not to pull the floats too tightly as this will pucker the fabric. By picking up the yarns over and under one another you will prevent them from tangling.

&weaving in

weaving in on a knit row

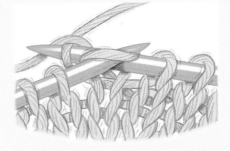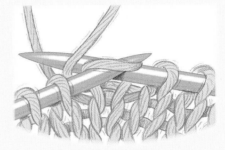

1 To weave in yarn on a knit stitch, insert the right-hand needle into the next stitch and lay the yarn to be woven in over the right-hand needle. Knit the stitch with the working yarn, taking it under the yarn not in use and making sure you do not catch this strand into the knitted stitch.

2 Knit the next stitch with the working yarn, taking it over the yarn being woven in. Continue like this, weaving the loose color over and under the working yarn until you need to use it again.

weaving in on a purl row

When there are more than four stitches between a color change, the floats are too long and this makes the fabric inflexible. The long strands can also catch when wearing the garment, particularly on the inside of a sleeve. By weaving in, the yarn not in use is caught up before the next color change, thus shortening the float. Sometimes, depending on the color pattern, a combination of both stranding and weaving in can be used.

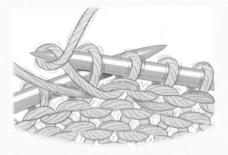

1 To weave in yarn on a purl stitch, insert the right-hand needle into the next stitch and lay the yarn to be woven in over the right-hand needle. Purl the stitch with the working yarn, taking it under the yarn not in use and making sure you do not catch this strand into the purled stitch.

2 Purl the next stitch with the working yarn, taking it over the yarn being woven in. Continue like this, weaving the loose color over and under the working yarn until you need to use it again.

seams

When you have completed the pieces of your knitting, you reach one of the most important stages. The way you finish your project determines how good your finished garment will look. There are different seam techniques, but the best by far is mattress or ladder stitch, which creates an invisible seam. It can be used on stockinette stitch, ribbing, garter stitch, and seed stitch.

The seam that I use for almost all sewing up is mattress stitch, which produces a wonderful invisible seam. It works well in any yarn, and makes a completely straight seam, as the same amount is taken up on each side—this also means that the knitted pieces should not need to be pinned together first. It is always worked on the right side of the fabric and is particularly useful for sewing seams on stripes and Fair Isle.

I use other types of seams less frequently, but they do have their uses. For instance, backstitch can sometimes be useful for sewing in a sleeve cap, to neatly ease in the fullness. It is also good for catching in loose strands of yarn on colorwork seams, where there can be a lot of short ends along the selvage. Just remember when using backstitch for seams on your knitting to ensure that you work in a completely straight line.

The grafting seam for joining two bound-off edges is handy for shoulder seams, while the seam for joining a bound-off edge with a side edge (selvage) is usually used when sewing a sleeve onto the body on a dropped shoulder style.

It is best to leave a long yarn tail at the casting-on stage to use for seams, so that the seaming yarn is already secured in place. If this is not possible, when first securing the thread for the seam, leave a length that can be darned in afterward. Sew all seams on knitting with a large blunt-ended yarn or tapestry needle to avoid splitting the yarn.

Before sewing side seams, sew the shoulder seams and sew on the sleeves, unless they are set-in sleeves. If there are any embellishments, such as applied pockets or embroidery, this is the time to sew them on, when you can lay the garment out flat.

seam techniques

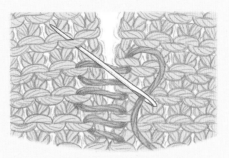

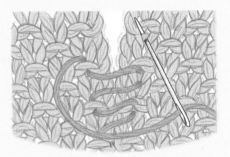

mattress stitch on stockinette stitch and double rib
With the right sides of the knitting facing you, insert the needle under the horizontal bar between the first stitch and next stitch. Then insert the needle under the same bar on the other piece. Continue to do this, pulling through the thread to form the seam.

mattress stitch on garter stitch
With the right sides of the knitting facing you, insert the needle through the bottom of the "knot" on the edge and then through the top of the corresponding "knot" on the opposite edge. Continue to do this from edge to edge, pulling through the yarn to form a flat seam.

mattress stitch on seed stitch
With the right sides of the knitting facing you, insert the needle under the horizontal bar between the first and second stitches on one side and through the top of the "knot" on the edge of the opposite side.

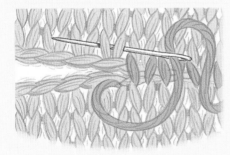

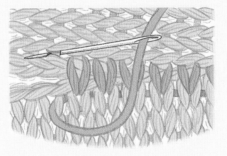

joining two bound-off edges (grafting)
1 With the bound-off edges butted together, bring the needle out in the center of the first stitch just below the bound-off edge on one piece. Insert the needle through the center of the first stitch on the other piece and out through the center of the next stitch.

2 Next, insert the needle through the center of the first stitch on the first piece again and out through the center of the stitch next to it. Continue in this way until the seam is completed.

joining bound-off and selvage edges
Bring the needle back to front through the center of the first stitch on the bound-off edge. Then insert it under one or two horizontal strands between the first and second stitches on the selvage and back through the center of the same bound-off stitch. Continue in this way until the seam is completed.

picking up stitches

When you are adding a border to your garment, such as front bands or a neckband, you usually pick up stitches around the edge. A border can be sewn on afterward but this method is neater. If you are picking up stitches along a long edge, a front band of a jacket for example, a long circular needle can be used so that you can fit all the stitches on. The pattern will usually tell you how many stitches to pick up.

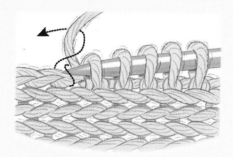

picking up stitches along a selvage
With the right side of the knitting facing, insert the knitting needle from front to back between the first and second stitches of the first row. Wrap the yarn around the needle and pull a loop through to a form a new stitch on the needle. Continue in this way along the edge of the knitting.

picking up stitches along a neck edge
On a neck edge, work along the straight edges as for a selvage. But along the curved edges, insert the needle through the center of the stitch below the shaping (to avoid large gaps) and pull a loop of yarn through to form a new stitch on the needle.

patterns

blanket
with decorative edge

measurements
Approximately 18^{1}/$_{4}$in x 27^{1}/$_{4}$in

materials
4 x 1^{3}/$_{4}$oz/50g balls Debbie Bliss Baby Cashmerino in lilac (M)
1 x 1^{3}/$_{4}$oz/50g ball Debbie Bliss Baby Cashmerino in each of silver (A) and chocolate (B)
Pair each of sizes 3 and 5 knitting needles

gauge
25 sts and 44 rows to 4in square over seed st using size 3 needles.

abbreviations
p2sso = pass 2 slipped sts over.
Also see page 25.

center panel

With size 3 needles and M, cast on 97 sts.
Seed st row K1, [p1, k1] to end.
This row forms the seed st and is repeated throughout.
Cont in seed st until panel measures 24^{1}/$_{2}$in.
Bind off.

top & bottom edgings

With size 5 needles and B, cast on 127 sts.
Change to A.
1st row (right side) K1, skp, k4, *skp, sl 2tog, k3tog, p2sso, k2tog, k4; rep from * to last 16 sts, skp, sl 2tog, k3tog, p2sso, k2tog, k4, k2tog, k1.
2nd row P7, *yo, p1, yo, p6; rep from * to last 8 sts, yo, p1, yo, p7.
3rd row K1, skp, k1, yo, *k2, skp, k1, k2tog, k2, yo; rep from * to last 4 sts, k1, k2tog, k1.
4th row P4, *yo, p2, yo, p3, yo, p2, yo, p1; rep from * to last 3 sts, p3.
5th row K1, skp, k1, yo, k1, *yo, skp, k1, sl 1, k2tog, psso, k1, k2tog, [yo, k1] 3 times; rep from * to last 14 sts, yo, skp, k1, sl 1, k2tog, psso, k1, k2tog, [yo, k1] twice, k2tog, k1.
6th row P to end.
7th row K1, skp, k3, *yo, sl 2tog, k3tog, p2sso, yo, k7; rep from * to last 11 sts, yo, sl 2tog, k3tog, p2sso, yo, k3, k2tog, k1.
K 3 rows. Bind off.

side edgings

With size 5 needles and B, cast on 205 sts.
Work as given for Top and Bottom Edgings.

to finish

Sew together corners of edging to form a square. Sew bound-off edges of edging to center section.

measurements
Approximately 17³/₄in x 27³/₄in

materials
1 x 1³/₄oz/50g ball Debbie Bliss Baby Cashmerino in gray (A)
2 x 1³/₄oz/50g balls Debbie Bliss Baby Cashmerino in each of pale peach (B), silver (C), and ecru (D)
Pair of size 3 knitting needles
Size 3 circular knitting needle

gauge
25 sts and 50 rows to 4in square over garter st using size 3 needles.

abbreviations
See page 25.

striped blanket

note
When working the stripe pattern in B, C, and D, do not break off yarn but carry the colors not in use up the side edge, making sure not to pull too tightly or the blanket will be distorted.

to make

With size 3 needles and A, cast on 107 sts.
K 4 rows.
Break off yarn.
Cont in garter st and work in stripe sequence as follows: 2 rows C, 2 rows B, 2 rows D.
The last 6 rows form the striped pattern and are repeated throughout.
Cont in pattern until work measures 27¹/₂in from cast-on edge.
Change to A and k 4 rows.
Bind off.

side edgings

With size 3 circular needle and A, pick up and k 117 sts along one side edge of blanket and k 4 rows.
Bind off.
Repeat on other side edge.

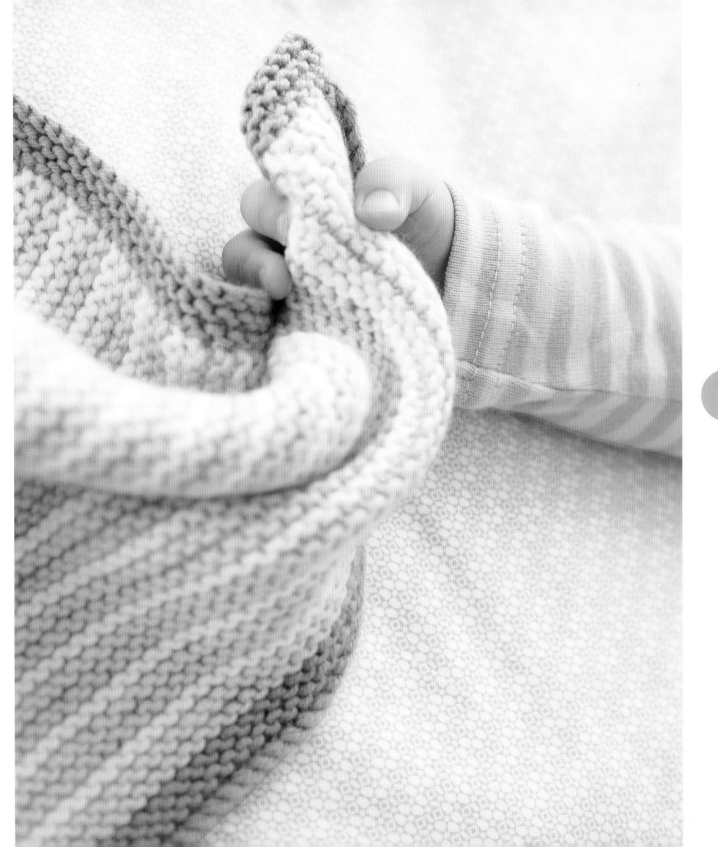

striped mouse

measurements
Approximately 7in tall

materials
Mouse 1 x 1³/₄oz/50g ball Debbie Bliss Baby Cashmerino in gray (A) and small amount of pale peach (B)
Pair of size 2 knitting needles
Small amount of embroidery thread for eyes, snout, and whiskers
Washable toy stuffing (see Safety Note on opposite page)
Dress Small amount of Debbie Bliss Baby Cashmerino in gray (A), pale peach (B), silver (C), and ecru (D)
Pair of size 3 knitting needles
Small button

gauge
25 sts and 40 rows to 4in square over St st using size 2 needles.

abbreviations
kfbf = knit into front, back, and front of next st.
s2togkp = slip 2 sts tog, k1, pass 2 slipped sts over.

safety note
Make sure you use a washable toy stuffing that is also non-flammable and nontoxic and adheres to toy safety regulations.

body

With size 2 needles and A, cast on 9 sts and p 1 row.
Next row (right side) [Kfb] 4 times, kfbf, [kfb] 4 times. 19 sts.
P 1 row.
Next row K5, M1, k1, M1, k8, M1, k1, M1, k4. 23 sts.
P 1 row.
Next row K6, M1, k1, M1, [k5, M1] twice, k1, M1, k5. 28 sts.
P 1 row.
Next row K14, M1, k1, M1, k13. 30 sts.
Beg with a p row, work 17 rows in St st.
Next row K5, k2tog, k1, ssk, k3, ssk, k1, k2tog, k3, k2tog, k1, ssk, k4. 24 sts.
P 1 row.
Next row K4, k2tog, k1, ssk, k2, ssk, k3, k2tog, k1, ssk, k3. 19 sts.
P 1 row.
Next row K3, k2tog, k1, ssk, k4, k2tog, k1, ssk, k2. 15 sts.
P 1 row.
Next row K2, k2tog, k1, ssk, k2, k2tog, k1, ssk, k1. 11 sts.
P 1 row.
Bind off.
Run a thread around the bound-off edge, pull together, and sew back seam, leaving a gap.
Stuff and sew up gap in seam.

head

With size 2 needles and A, cast on 4 sts and p 1 row.
Next row [Kfb] 3 times, k1. 7 sts.
P 1 row.
Next row K1, [M1, k2, M1, k1] to end. 11 sts.
Beg with a p row, work 3 rows in St st.
Next row K1, [M1, k3] 3 times, M1, k1.
P 1 row.
Next row K1, M1, k to last st, M1, k1.
Next row P1, M1, p to last st, M1, p1.
Next row K1, [M1, k3] twice, M1, k5, [M1, k3] twice, M1, k1. 25 sts.
Place markers at each end of last row.
Beg with a p row, work 6 rows.
Next row P4, p2tog, p13, p2tog tbl, p4.
Next row K14, ssk, turn.
Next row Sl 1, p5, p2tog, turn.
Next row Sl 1, k5, ssk, turn.
Rep last 2 rows 6 times more.
Bind off purlwise, working last 2 sts tog.
Sew seam from point of snout to markers, and stuff head.

outer ears (make 2)

With size 2 needles and A, cast on 7 sts.
Beg with a k row, work 4 rows in St st.
Next row Ssk, k3, k2tog.
P 1 row.
Next row Ssk, k1, k2tog.
Next row P3tog and finish off.

inner ears (make 2)

With size 2 needles and B, cast on 6 sts.
Beg with a k row, work 3 rows in St st.
Next row P2tog, p2, p2tog tbl.
Next row Ssk, k2tog.
Next row P3tog and finish off.

arms (make 2)

With size 2 needles and A, cast on 4 sts and p 1 row.
Next row [Kfb] 3 times, k1. 7 sts.
P 1 row.
Next row [K1, M1, k2, M1] twice, k1. 11 sts.
Beg with a p row, work 3 rows in St st.
Next row K3, ssk, k1, k2tog, k3. 9 sts.
Beg with a p row, work 13 rows in St st.
Place markers at each end of last row.
Next row K1, ssk, k3, k2tog, k1. 7 sts.
P 1 row.
Next row K1, ssk, k1, k2tog, k1. 5 sts.
P 1 row.
Next row K1, s2togkp, k1. 3 sts.
P 1 row.
Next row S2togkp. 1 st.
Finish off.
Sew arm seam, from cast-on edge to markers, and stuff.

legs (make 2)

With size 2 needles and A, cast on 8 sts and p 1 row.
Next row (right side) [Kfb] 7 times, k1. 15 sts.
P 1 row.
Next row K1, M1, k4, [M1, k1] 6 times, k3, M1, k1. 23 sts.
Beg with a p row, work 3 rows in St st.
Next row K9, k2tog, k1, ssk, k9. 21 sts.
P 1 row.
Next row K8, k2tog, k1, ssk, k8. 19 sts.
Next row P7, p2tog tbl, p1, p2tog, p7. 17 sts.
Next row K7, s2togkp, k7. 15 sts.
P 1 row.
Next row K5, ssk, k1, k2tog, k5. 13 sts.
Beg with a p row, work 23 rows in St st.

Next row K1, [ssk] twice, k3, [k2tog] twice, k1. 9 sts.
P 1 row.
Next row K1, ssk, k3, k2tog, k1. 7 sts.
Next row P1, p2tog, p1, p2tog tbl, p1.
Break off yarn, thread through rem 5 sts, pull together, and secure.
Sew leg seam, leaving a gap for stuffing. Stuff foot and leg, then sew up gap in seam.

tail

With size 2 needles and A, cast on 25 sts.
Bind off.

to finish

Sew ears together in pairs of inner and outer ear pieces and sew to head. Using embroidery thread, work eyes, snout, and whiskers. Sew head to body, gathering slightly around neck edge. Sew arms in place around open edge. Sew on legs and tail.

dress

With size 3 needles and A, cast on 48 sts.
K 1 row.
*Change to C and k 2 rows.
Change to B and k 2 rows.
Change to D and k 2 rows.
Rep from * 3 times more.
Change to C and work as follows:
Next row (right side) K10, [k2tog] 14 times, k10. 34 sts.
Divide for front and back yokes
Next row (wrong side) K6 (for right back), bind off 4 sts (for armhole), with one st on needle after bind-off, k next 13 sts (for front), bind off 4 sts (for armhole), k to end (for left back).
Change to B and work as follows:
On first set of 6 sts (left back), k 13 rows.
Bind off knitwise.
With right side facing, rejoin B to 14 sts of front, k 13 rows.
Bind off knitwise.
With right side facing, rejoin B to 6 sts of right back, k 13 rows.
Bind off knitwise and leave a long length of yarn.
With the long length of yarn, make a small button loop on edge of right back.
Sew back seam from cast-on edge to beg of yoke.
Sew button to left back.

reversible
blanket

measurements
Approximately 39¹/₄in x 39¹/₄in

materials
13 x 1³/₄oz/50g balls Debbie Bliss Cashmerino Aran in each of stone (A) and blue (B)
1 x 1³/₄oz/50g ball Debbie Bliss Cashmerino Aran in chocolate (C) for blanket stitch detail
Size 8 circular knitting needle

gauge
18 sts and 24 rows to 4in square over St st using size 8 needles.

abbreviations
See page 25.

first side

With size 8 circular needle and A, cast on 175 sts.
Working back and forth in rows throughout, k 5 rows.
Work in patt as follows:
1st row (right side) K7, [p1, k7] to last 8 sts, p1, k7.
2nd row K3, p3, [k1, p1, k1, p5] to last 9 sts, k1, p1, k1, p3, k3.
3rd row K5, [p1, k3] to last 6 sts, p1, k5.
4th row K3, p1, [k1, p5, k1, p1] to last 3 sts, k3.
5th row K3, p1, [k7, p1] to last 3 sts, k3.
6th row Rep 4th row.
7th row Rep 3rd row.
8th row Rep 2nd row.
These 8 rows form the patt with garter st edging.
Cont in patt until work measures 38^1/$_2$in from cast-on edge, ending with a right-side row.
K 5 rows.
Bind off.

second side

With size 8 circular needle and B, cast on 175 sts.
Working back and forth in rows throughout, k 5 rows.
Beg patt as follows:
1st row (right side) K3, [p1, k7] to last 4 sts, p1, k3.
2nd row K3, [p7, k1] to last 4 sts, p1, k3.
3rd row K5, [p1, k7] to last 10 sts, p1, k9.
4th row K3, p5, [k1, p7] to last 7 sts, k1, p3, k3.
5th row K7, [p1, k7] to end.
6th row K3, p3, [k1, p7] to last 9 sts, k1, p5, k3.
7th row K9, [p1, k7] to last 6 sts, p1, k5.
8th row K3, p1, [k1, p7] to last 3 sts, k3.
These 8 rows form the patt with garter st edging.
Cont in patt until work measures 38^1/$_2$in from cast-on edge, ending with a right-side row.
K 5 rows.
Bind off.

to finish

With wrong sides together, sew first and second sides together around the outer edge.
With two strands of C held together, work blanket stitch around the edges.

booties
with blanket stitch detail

size
To fit ages 3–6 months

materials
1 x 1³/₄oz/50g ball Debbie Bliss Baby Cashmerino in pale blue (A) and small amount of chocolate (B) for blanket stitch detail
Pair of size 2 knitting needles

gauge
28 sts and 50 rows to 4in square over garter st using size 2 needles.

abbreviations
See page 25.

booties (make 2)

With size 2 needles and A, cast on 36 sts.
K 36 rows.
Shape instep
Next row K23, turn.
Next row K10, turn.
Work 24 rows in garter st on center 10 sts.
Next row K1, skp, k to last 3 sts, k2tog, k1.
K 1 row.
Break off yarn.
With right side facing, rejoin yarn at base of instep and pick up and k 13 sts along side of instep, k across center 8 sts, then pick up and k 13 sts along other side of instep. 34 sts.
Beg with a p row, work 5 rows in St st on these 34 sts.
Next row [K next st tog with corresponding st 5 rows below] 34 times, then k to end.
Next row K to end. 60 sts.
K 12 rows.
Beg with a k row, work 7 rows in St st.
Next row [P next st tog with corresponding st 7 rows below] to end.
Break off yarn.
Shape sole
Next row Slip first 25 sts onto right-hand needle, rejoin yarn and k 10 sts, turn.
Next row K9, k2tog, turn.
Rep last row until 20 sts rem.
Bind off.

to finish

Sew back seam. With back seam at center of bound-off edge, sew heel seam.
With B, work blanket stitch around edge of turned down cuff.

rabbit
with blanket stitch detail

measurements
Approximately 10in tall

materials
2 x 1³/₄oz/50g balls Debbie Bliss Baby Cashmerino in pale blue (A), and small amount in each of chocolate (B) for embroidery and ecru (C) for pompon tail
Pair of size 2 knitting needles
Washable toy stuffing (see Safety Note on page 47)
4in square of chocolate felt

gague
28 sts and 58 rows to 4in square over garter st using size 2 needles.

abbreviations
yb = yarn to back of work between two needles.
yf = yarn to front of work between two needles.
s2togkp = slip 2 sts tog, k1, pass 2 slipped sts over.
Also see page 25.

body back

(Worked from neck edge.)
With size 2 needles and A, cast on 12 sts and k 1 row.
Shape shoulders
Next row [K2, M1] twice, k4, [M1, k2] twice. 16 sts.
K 1 row.
Next row K3, M1, k2, M1, k6, M1, k2, M1, k3. 20 sts.
K 5 rows.
Next row K1, M1, k to last st, M1, k1. 22 sts.
K 5 rows.**
Rep the last 6 rows 5 times more. 32 sts.
Shape base
Next row K1, [ssk, k11, k2tog] twice, k1. 28 sts.
K 1 row.
Next row K1, [ssk, k9, k2tog] twice, k1. 24 sts.
K 1 row.
***Next row** K1, [ssk, k7, k2tog] twice, k1. 20 sts.
K 1 row.
Cont to dec 4 sts in this way on every alt row until 8 sts rem.
Next row K1, sl 1, k2tog, psso, k3tog, k1. 4 sts.
Next row [K2tog] twice. 2 sts.
Next row K2tog and finish off.

body front

Work as Body Back to **.
Next row K1, M1, k to last st, M1, k1. 24 sts.
K 5 rows.
Next row K1, M1, k10, M1, k2, M1, k10, M1, k1. 28 sts.
K 5 rows.
Next row K1, M1, k10, M1, k6, M1, k10, M1, k1. 32 sts.
K 5 rows.
Next row K1, M1, k to last st, M1, k1. 34 sts.
K 5 rows.
Rep the last 6 rows once more. 36 sts.
Next row K1, ssk, k6, [ssk, k5, k2tog] twice, k6, k2tog, k1. 30 sts.
K 1 row.
Next row K1, ssk, k5, [ssk, k3, k2tog] twice, k5, k2tog, k1. 24 sts.
K 1 row.
Now work as Body Back from *** to end.

head

With size 2 needles and A, cast on 4 sts.
1st row K.
2nd row K1, [M1, k1] to end. 7 sts.
Rep the last 2 rows once more. 13 sts.
5th, 7th, 9th, and 11th rows K.
6th row [K1, M1, k5, M1] twice, k1. 17 sts.
8th row K1, M1, k6, M1, k3, M1, k6, M1, k1. 21 sts.
10th row K1, M1, k7, M1, k5, M1, k7, M1, k1. 25 sts.
12th row K1, M1, k8, M1, k7, M1, k8, M1, k1. 29 sts.
K 2 rows.
15th row K2, [ssk, k1] 3 times, k8, [k2tog, k1] 3 times, k1. 23 sts.
16th row K4, M1, k3, M1, k9, M1, k3, M1, k4. 27 sts.
K 3 rows.
20th row [K4, M1] twice, k11, [M1, k4] twice. 31 sts.
K 3 rows.
24th row K4, M1, k5, M1, k13, M1, k5, M1, k4. 35 sts.
K 1 row.
26th row K4, M1, k6, M1, k15, M1, k6, M1, k4. 39 sts.
K 1 row.
28th row K4, M1, k7, M1, k17, M1, k7, M1, k4. 43 sts.
K 1 row.
30th row K3, [M1, k4] 3 times, M1, k13, M1, [k4, M1] 3 times, k3. 51 sts.
K 12 rows.
43rd row K9, k2tog, [k8, k2tog] 4 times. 46 sts.
K 1 row.
45th row K8, k2tog, [k7, k2tog] 4 times. 41 sts.
K 1 row.
47th row K7, k2tog, [k6, k2tog] 4 times. 36 sts.
K 1 row.

Dec 5 sts in this way on next row and 4 foll alt rows. 11 sts.
K 1 row.
Next row Sl 1, k2tog, psso, [k2tog] 4 times. 5 sts.
Break off yarn, thread through rem sts, pull together, and secure.
Sew seam, leaving a gap. Stuff carefully and sew up gap in seam.

ears (make 2)

With size 2 needles and A, cast on 15 sts.
K 1 row.
**Next 2 rows K2, yf, sl 1, turn, yf, sl 1, yb, k2.
Next 2 rows K4, yf, sl 1, turn, yf, sl 1, yb, k4.
Next 2 rows K6, yf, sl 1, turn, yf, sl 1, yb, k6.
Next 2 rows K7, yf, sl 1, turn, yf, sl 1, yb, k7.
K 1 row across all sts.**
Rep from ** to ** once more.
K 48 rows.
Next row K1, skp, k to last 3 sts, k2tog, k1.
K 3 rows.
Rep the last 4 rows once more. 11 sts.
Next row K1, skp, k to last 3 sts, k2tog, k1.
K 1 row.
Rep the last 2 rows twice more. 5 sts.
Next row K1, s2togkp, k1.
Next row S2togkp and finish off.
Fold cast-on edge in half and sew two layers of cast-on edge together.
With B, work blanket stitch around edge of each ear.

legs (make 2)

With size 2 needles and A, cast on 15 sts.
K 1 row.
2nd row K1, M1, k4, M1, k1, M1, k3, M1, k1, M1, k4, M1, k1. 21 sts.
K 1 row.
4th row K1, M1, k6, M1, k2, M1, k3, M1, k2, M1, k6, M1, k1. 27 sts.
K 1 row.
6th row K9, M1, k3, [M1, k1] 3 times, M1, k3, M1, k9. 33 sts.
K 9 rows.
16th row K12, ssk, k5, k2tog, k12. 31 sts.
K 1 row.
18th row K12, ssk, k3, k2tog, k12. 29 sts.
K 1 row.
20th row K12, ssk, k1, k2tog, k12. 27 sts.
K 1 row.
22nd row K11, ssk, k1, k2tog, k11. 25 sts.
K 1 row.
24th row K10, ssk, k1, k2tog, k10. 23 sts.
K 1 row.

26th row K9, ssk, k1, k2tog, k9. 21 sts.

K 28 rows.

56th row K4, ssk, k9, k2tog, k4. 19 sts.

K 1 row.

58th row K4, ssk, k7, k2tog, k4. 17 sts.

K 1 row.

60th row K2, ssk, k2tog, k5, ssk, k2tog, k2. 13 sts.

K 1 row.

62nd row K1, ssk, k2tog, s2togkp, ssk, k2tog, k1. 7 sts.

K 1 row.

64th row K1, ssk, k1, k2tog, k1. 5 sts.

Break off yarn, thread through rem sts, pull together, and secure.

arms (make 2)

With size 2 needles and A, cast on 7 sts.

K 1 row.

2nd row [K1, M1, k2, M1] twice, k1. 11 sts.

K 1 row.

4th row K1, M1, [k3, M1] 3 times, k1. 15 sts.

K 1 row.

6th row K1, M1, k4, M1, k5, M1, k4, M1, k1. 19 sts.

K 1 row.

8th row K1, M1, k17, M1, k1. 21 sts.

K 1 row.

10th row K1, M1, k7, ssk, k1, k2tog, k7, M1, k1. 21 sts.

K 1 row.

Rep the last 2 rows once more.

14th row K8, ssk, k1, k2tog, k8. 19 sts.

K 1 row.

16th row K7, ssk, k1, k2tog, k7. 17 sts.

K 24 rows.

41st row K2, ssk, k2tog, k5, ssk, k2tog, k2. 13 sts.

K 1 row.

43rd row K1, ssk, k2tog, s2togkp, ssk, k2tog, k1. 7 sts.

K 1 row.

45th row K1, ssk, k1, k2tog, k1. 5 sts.

Break off yarn, thread through rem sts, pull together, and secure.

to finish

Sew body back to body front leaving neck edge open. Stuff firmly and run a thread around neck edge, pull together slightly, and secure. Sew ears to head. Embroider facial features with B. Sew head to body at neck. Fold each arm and each leg in half, and sew seam leaving a gap. Stuff legs and arms firmly and sew up gaps. Sew arms and legs to body. Using the little bear sole template on page 120, cut two soles from chocolate felt and sew to feet. With B, work three lines on feet for toes and on arms for paws. Make a small pompom in C and sew to body for tail.

measurements
Approximately 30in x 38in

materials
10 x 1³/₄oz/50g balls Debbie Bliss Cashmerino Aran in each of charcoal gray (A) and mid gray (B)
1 x 1³/₄oz/50g ball Debbie Bliss Cashmerino Aran in silver (C)
Size 8 circular knitting needle

gauge
20 sts and 26 rows to 4in square over patt using size 8 needles.

abbreviations
See page 25.

running stitch blanket

first side

With size 8 circular needle and A, cast on 151 sts.
1st row K1, [p1, k3] to last 2 sts, p1, k1.
2nd row Purl.
These 2 rows form the broken rib patt and are repeated throughout.
Cont in patt until work measures approximately 38in, ending with a 1st row and making sure you have enough yarn for binding off and sewing seams.
Bind off knitwise.

second side

Make exactly as for First Side, but using B.

to finish

Work contrasting running stitch in C on both pieces of blanket using the vertical lines as a guide and running the yarn under every alternate purl st. With wrong sides together, sew first and second sides together, overcast stitching with A around the outer edge.

measurements
Approximately 22$\frac{1}{2}$in x 29$\frac{1}{2}$in

materials
5 x 1$\frac{3}{4}$oz/50g balls Debbie Bliss Baby Cashmerino in silver (M)
1 x 1$\frac{3}{4}$oz/50g ball Debbie Bliss Baby Cashmerino in each of camel (A) and stone (B)
Small amount of chocolate yarn (C) for embroidery
Size 3 circular knitting needle

gauge
25 sts and 34 rows to 4in square over St st using size 3 needles.

abbreviations
See page 25.

teddy blanket

to make

With size 3 circular needle and M, cast on 144 sts.
K 9 rows.
First line of motifs
1st row (right side) K39, [p1, k1] 16 times, p1, k33, [p1, k1] 16 times, p1, k6.
2nd row K6, [p1, k1] 16 times, p35, [k1, p1] 15 times, k1, p34, k6.
3rd–9th rows Rep the 1st and 2nd rows 3 times more and the 1st row again.
10th row (wrong side) K6, [p1, k1] 16 times, p8, work across 1st row of Chart on page 71 (reading this chart row—a wrong-side row—from left to right), p8, [k1, p1] 15 times, k1, p8, work across 1st row of Chart, p7, k6.
11th row K13, work across 2nd row of Chart (reading this chart row—a right-side row—from right to left), k7, [p1, k1] 16 times, p1, k7, work across 2nd row of Chart, k7, [p1, k1] 16 times, p1, k6.
Working correct Chart rows, rep the last 2 rows 10 times more, so completing the Chart.
32nd row K6, [p1, k1] 16 times, p35, [k1, p1] 15 times, k1, p34, k6.
33rd–40th rows Rep 1st and 2nd rows 4 times.
Second line of motifs
1st row (right side) K6, [p1, k1] 16 times, p1, k33, p1, [k1, p1] 16 times, k39.
2nd row K6, p34, [k1, p1] 15 times, k1, p35, [k1, p1] 16 times, k6.
3rd–9th rows Rep the 1st and 2nd rows 3 times more and the first row again.

10th row (wrong side) K6, p7, work across 1st row of Chart, p8, [k1, p1] 15 times, k1, p8, work across 1st row of Chart, p8, [k1, p1] 16 times, k6.

11th row K6, [p1, k1] 16 times, p1, k7, work across 2nd row of Chart, k7, [p1, k1] 16 times, p1, k7, work across 2nd row of Chart, k13.

Working correct Chart rows, rep the last 2 rows 10 times more, so completing the Chart.

32nd row K6, p34, [k1, p1] 15 times, k1, p35, [k1, p1] 16 times, k6.

33rd–40th rows Rep 1st and 2nd rows 4 times.

Third to sixth lines of motifs

Rep 1st and 2nd lines twice more.

K 10 rows.

Bind off.

to finish

With C, embroider features, using straight stitches.

teddy blanket chart

● When working from Chart, use a separate small ball of yarn for each color area and twist yarns at color change to avoid holes.
● Use A and B for bear motifs in alternate squares.

27 sts

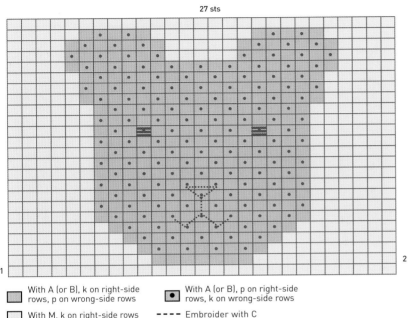

1   2

| | With A (or B), k on right-side rows, p on wrong-side rows | | With A (or B), p on right-side rows, k on wrong-side rows |
| | With M, k on right-side rows and and p on wrong-side rows | - - - - | Embroider with C |

teddy slippers chart

Read right-side rows from right to left and wrong-side rows from left to right. When working from chart use a separate ball of yarn for each color area and twist yarns at color change on wrong side to avoid a hole.

With M, p on right-side rows, k on wrong-side rows
With M, k on right-side rows, p on wrong-side rows
With A, k on right-side rows, p on wrong-side rows
With A, p on right-side rows, k on wrong-side rows

Embroider with C - - - -

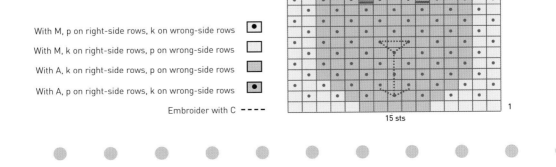

1

15 sts

size
To fit ages 3–6 months

materials
1 x 1³⁄₄oz/50g ball Debbie Bliss Baby Cashmerino in each of silver (M) and camel (A)
Small amount of chocolate yarn (B) for embroidery
Pair of size 2 knitting needles

gauge
27 sts and 46 rows to 4in square over seed st using size 2 needles.

abbreviations
See page 25.

teddy slippers

to make

With size 2 needles and M, cast on 31 sts.
1st row (wrong side) P1, [k1, p1] to end.
This row **sets** the seed st.
Next row Work 2 tog, seed st to end.
Rep the last row 23 times more. **7 sts.**
Next row Inc in first st, seed st to end.
Rep the last row 9 times more. **17 sts.**
Next row (right side) Inc in first st, work across 1st row of Chart on page 71 (reading this chart row—a right-side row—from right to left), seed st last st.
Next row Inc in first st, work across 2nd row of Chart (reading this chart row—a wrong-side row—from left to right), seed st 2.
These 2 rows set the position of the Chart.
Cont in seed st with chart and inc one st at beg of next 12 rows. **31 sts.**
Next row Work 2 tog, seed st to end.
Rep the last row 27 times more. **3 sts.**
Bind off.

to finish

Embroider eyes, nose, and mouth with B.
Fold bound-off edge and two corners into center, and sew seams.
Bring both ends of edging to center, and sew seams.

triangle edge top

sizes and measurements
To fit ages 3–6 (6–9: 9–12: 12–18) months
finished measurements
Chest 20 (22: 23^1/$_2$: 25^1/$_2$)in
Length to shoulder 9^1/$_2$ (10^1/$_4$: 11: 12^1/$_2$)in
Sleeve length 6 (6^3/$_4$: 7^1/$_2$: 8^3/$_4$)in

materials
3 (4: 4: 5) x 1^3/$_4$oz/50g balls Debbie Bliss Baby Cashmerino in lilac (M) and
small amount of aubergine (C) for edging
Pair each of sizes 2 and 3 knitting needles
One size 3 double-pointed knitting needle
3 buttons

gauge
25 sts and 34 rows to 4in square over St st using size 3 needles.

abbreviations
See page 25.

back

With size 2 needles and M, cast on 92 (98: 104: 110) sts.

Next row (wrong side) K to end.

Next row K39 (42: 45: 48), sl 1, k12, sl 1, k39 (42: 45: 48).

Next row K32 (35: 38: 41), sl 1, k26, sl 1, k32 (35: 38: 41).

Rep the last 2 rows twice more.

Change to size 3 needles.

Next row (right side) K39 (42: 45: 48), sl 1, k12, sl 1, k39 (42: 45: 48).

Next row P32 (35: 38: 41), sl 1, p26, sl 1, p32 (35: 38: 41).

Rep the last 2 rows until back measures 5^1/$_2$ (6: 6^1/$_4$: 7^1/$_2$)in, ending with a wrong-side row.

Shape armholes

Bind off 4 sts at beg of next 2 rows. 84 (90: 96: 102) sts.

Work 14 rows more.

Next row (right side) K29 (32: 35: 38), bind off 26, k to end. 58 (64: 70: 76) sts.

Work even until back measures 9^1/$_2$ (10^1/$_4$: 11: 12^1/$_2$)in, ending with a wrong-side row.

Shape shoulders

Bind off 7 (8: 9: 10) sts at beg of next 4 rows.

Leave rem 30 (32: 34: 36) sts on a spare needle.

front

With size 2 needles and M, cast on 66 (72: 78: 84) sts.

K 7 rows.

Beg with a k row, work in St st until front measures 5^1/$_2$ (6: 6^1/$_4$: 7^1/$_2$)in, ending with a wrong-side row.

Shape armholes

Bind off 4 sts at beg of next 2 rows. 58 (64: 70: 76) sts.

Front opening

Next row (right side) K29 (32: 35: 38), cast on 4 sts onto right-hand needle after sts just worked, then turn and work on these 33 (36: 39: 42) sts for first side of front opening.

1st row K2, p to end.

2nd row K to end.

Rep the last 2 rows 10 times more and the first row again.

Shape neck

Next row (right side) K to last 11 (12: 13: 14) sts and leave these sts on a holder, turn and work on rem 22 (24: 26: 28) sts.

Dec 1 st at neck edge on every row until 14 (16: 18: 20) sts rem.

Work even until front measures the same as Back to shoulder, ending at armhole edge.

Shape shoulder

Bind off 7 (8: 9: 10) sts at beg of next row.

Work 1 row.

Bind off rem 7 (8: 9: 10) sts.

With right side facing, rejoin yarn to rem 29 (32: 35: 38) sts.

1st row K to end.

2nd row P26 (29: 32: 33), k2, M1, k to end.

3rd–6th rows Rep 1st and 2nd rows twice more.

7th row (buttonhole row) K2, k2tog, yo, k to end.

8th row P26 (29: 32: 33), k2, k into front and back of yo, k3.
9th and 10th rows Rep 1st and 2nd rows.
11th row Bind off 5 sts, k to end.
Rep 2nd–11th rows once more then 2nd–4th rows again.
Shape neck
Next row (right side) K9 (10: 11: 12) and leave these sts on a holder, k to end.
Dec 1 st at neck edge on every row until 14 (16: 18: 20) sts rem.
Work even until front measures same as Back to shoulder, ending at armhole edge.
Shape shoulder
Bind off 7 (8: 9: 10) sts at beg of next row.
Work 1 row.
Bind off rem 7 (8: 9: 10) sts.

sleeves

With size 2 needles and M, cast on 35 (37: 41: 43) sts.
K 7 rows.
Change to size 3 needles.
Beg with a k row, work in St st.
Work 2 rows.
Next row (inc row) K3, M1, k to last 3 sts, M1, k3.
Work 5 rows.
Rep the last 6 rows 5 (6: 7: 9) times more and the inc row again. 49 (53: 59: 65) sts.
Work even until sleeve measures 6 (6³/₄: 7¹/₂: 8³/₄)in, ending with a wrong-side row.
Place markers at each end of last row.
Work 6 rows more.
Bind off.

neckband

Sew shoulder seams.
With right side facing, size 2 needles, and M, slip 9 (10: 11: 12) sts from right front holder onto a needle, pick up and k 12 (13: 14: 15) sts up right front neck, k 30 (32: 34: 36) sts from back neck holder, pick up and k 12 (13: 14: 15) sts down left front neck, then k 11 (12: 13: 14) sts from left front holder. 74 (80: 86: 92) sts.
Next row (wrong side) K to last 3 sts, M1, k3.
Next row (buttonhole row) K2, k2tog, yo, k to end.
Next row K to last 4 sts, k into front and back of yo, k3.
Next row K to end.
Next row K to last 5 sts, M1, k5.
Bind off.

front edging

Cut a 2¹/₈yd length of contrasting yarn (C).
With right side facing and using size 3 double-pointed needle, starting halfway along length of yarn, pick up and k 6 sts along row ends of first point, *slip sts to other end of needle, using other half of yarn, bind off 5 sts, with one st on needle, use double-pointed needle and first half of yarn, pick up and k 5 sts along bound-off edge of point, slip sts to other end of needle, using other half of yarn **, bind off 5 sts, with one st on needle, pick up and k 5 sts along row ends of next point; rep from * once more, then from * to **, bind off rem 6 sts.

to finish

Matching center of bound-off edge of sleeve to shoulder, sew sleeves into armholes, with row ends above markers sewn to sts bound off at underarm. Sew side and sleeve seams. Sew cast-on sts for button band behind buttonhole band. Sew on buttons. Fold bound-off sts at center back to form a box pleat on wrong side of work, and sew in place.

size
To fit ages 3–6 months

materials
1 x 1³/₄oz/50g ball Debbie Bliss Baby Cashmerino in lilac (M) and small amount of aubergine (C) for edging
Pair of size 2 knitting needles
One size 2 double-pointed knitting needle

gauge
25 sts and 34 rows to 4in square over St st using size 3 needles.

abbreviations
See page 25.

triangle edge
booties

to make

With size 2 needles and M, cast on 36 sts.
K 1 row.
1st row (right side) K1, yo, k16, yo, [k1, yo] twice, k16, yo, k1.
2nd and all wrong-side rows K to end, working k1 tbl into each yo of previous row.
3rd row K2, yo, k16, yo, k2, yo, k3, yo, k16, yo, k2.
5th row K3, yo, k16, yo, [k4, yo] twice, k16, yo, k3.
7th row K4, yo, k16, yo, k5, yo, k6, yo, k16, yo, k4.
9th row K5, yo, k16, yo, [k7, yo] twice, k16, yo, k5.
11th row K22, yo, k8, yo, k9, yo, k22. 64 sts.
12th row Rep 2nd row.
Beg with a k row, work 9 rows St st.
K 3 rows.
Shape instep
Next row K36, skp, turn.
Next row Sl 1, p8, p2tog, turn.
Next row Sl 1, k8, skp, turn.
Rep the last 2 rows 7 times more, then work first of the 2 rows again.
Next row Sl 1, k to end.
Next row P17, p2tog tbl, p8, p2tog, p17. 44 sts.
Dec row [K3, k2tog] 4 times, k4, [skp, k3] 4 times. 36 sts.
Beg with a p row, work 15 rows in St st.
K 6 rows.
Bind off.

edging

With size 2 needles and M, cast on 3 sts.
1st row K2, M1, k to end.
2nd row K to end.
3rd–9th rows Rep 1st and 2nd rows 3 times more and the first row again. 8 sts.
10th row Bind off 5 sts, k to end.
Rep 1st–10th rows 5 times more, then 1st–9th rows once more.
Bind off all sts.
Cut a 3¹/₄yd length of contrasting yarn (C).
With right side facing and using size 2 double-pointed needle, starting halfway along length of yarn, pick up and k 6 sts along row ends of first point, *slip sts to other end of needle, using other half of yarn, bind off 5 sts, with one st on needle, use double-pointed needle and first half of yarn pick up and k 5 sts along bound-off edge of point, slip sts to other end of needle, using other half of yarn **, bind off 5 sts, with one st on needle, pick up and k 5 sts along row ends of next point; rep from * 5 times more, then from * to **, bind off rem 6 sts.

to finish

Sew edging to bound-off sts of bootie. Sew back and sole seam. Fold edging to right side.

measurements
Approximately 26in x 26in

materials
10 x 1³/₄oz/50g balls Debbie Bliss Cashmerino Aran in ecru
Pair of size 8 knitting needles
Size 8 circular knitting needle

gauge
18 sts and 36 rows to 4in square over garter st using size 8 needles.

abbreviations
See page 25.

hooded blanket

main part

With size 8 circular needle, cast on 3 sts and k 1 row.
Next row (right side) [K1, M1] twice, k1.
Next row K5.
Next row K2, M1, k1, M1, k2.
Next row K to end.
Next row K2, M1, k to last 2 sts, M1, k2.
Rep the last 2 rows until side edge measures 26in, ending with a wrong-side row.
Next row K1, skp, k to last 3 sts, k2tog, k1.
Next row K to end.
Rep the last 2 rows until 5 sts rem, ending with a wrong-side row.
Next row K1, s1 1, k2tog, psso, k1.
Bind off rem 3 sts.

hood

With size 8 needles, cast on 75 sts and k 1 row.
Next row (right side) K1, skp, k to last 3 sts, k2tog, k1.
Next row K to end.
Rep the last 2 rows until 5 sts rem, ending with a wrong-side row.
Next row K1, s1 1, k2tog, psso, k1.
Bind off rem 3 sts.

to finish

Sew hood to corner of main part.

size
To fit age 3–6 months

materials
1 x 1³/₄oz/50g ball Debbie Bliss Baby Cashmerino in pale blue
Pair of size 2 knitting needles
2 buttons

gauge
28 sts and 37 rows to 4in square over St st using size 2 needles.

abbreviations
See page 25.

sandals

right sandal

With size 2 needles, cast on 36 sts.

K 1 row.

1st row (right side) K1, yo, k16, yo, [k1, yo] twice, k16, yo, k1.

2nd and all wrong side rows K to end, working k1 tbl into each yo of previous row.

3rd row K2, yo, k16, yo, k2, yo, k3, yo, k16, yo, k2.

5th row K3, yo, k16, yo, [k4, yo] twice, k16, yo, k3.

7th row K4, yo, k16, yo, k5, yo, k6, yo, k16, yo, k4.

9th row K5, yo, k16, yo, [k7, yo] twice, k16, yo, k5.

11th row K22, yo, k8, yo, k9, yo, k22. 64 sts.

12th row Rep 2nd row.

Beg with a k row, work 7 rows in St st.

Next row [P next st tog with corresponding st 7 rows below] to end.

Beg with a k row, work 8 rows in St st.

Shape instep

Next row K36, skp, turn.

Next row Sl 1, p8, p2tog, turn.

Next row Sl 1, k8, skp, turn.

Rep the last 2 rows 7 times more, then work the first of the 2 rows again.

Next row Sl 1, k to end.

Next row K17, k2tog, p8, skp, k17. 44 sts.

Next row K24, turn.

Next row P4, turn.

Next row K4, turn.

Work 2¼in in St st on these 4 sts only for front strap.

Bind off these 4 sts.

With right side facing, rejoin yarn at base of strap, pick up and k 15 sts along side edge of strap, then turn and bind off 26 sts knitwise, leave rem 9 sts on a holder.

With right side facing, rejoin yarn to top of other side of strap, pick up and k 15 sts along side edge of strap, then k rem 20 sts.

Next row K9, bind off rem 26 sts knitwise.

Sew sole and back heel seam.

With right side facing and size 2 needles, k across 18 sts along heel for ankle strap.**

Next row Cast on 22 sts at beg of row, k to end, cast on 4 sts and turn.

Buttonhole row K to last 3 sts, yo, k2tog, k1.

K 2 rows.

Bind off.

Fold front strap over ankle strap and slip stitch bound-off edge in place.

Sew on button.

left sandal

Work as given for Right Sandal to **.

Next row Cast on 4 sts at beg of row, k to end, cast on 22 sts and turn.

Buttonhole row K1, skp, yo, k to end.

Complete as Right Sandal.

picot booties

size
To fit age 3–6 months

materials
1 x 1³/₄oz/50g ball Debbie Bliss Baby Cashmerino in ecru
Pair of size 2 knitting needles
2 buttons

gauge
28 sts and 37 rows to 4in square over St st using size 2 needles.

abbreviations
See page 25.

right bootie

With size 2 needles, cast on 36 sts.
K 1 row.
1st row (right side) K1, yo, k16, yo, [k1, yo] twice, k16, yo, k1.
2nd and all wrong side rows K to end, working k1 tbl into each yo of previous row.
3rd row K2, yo, k16, yo, k2, yo, k3, yo, k16, yo, k2.
5th row K3, yo, k16, yo, [k4, yo] twice, k16, yo, k3.
7th row K4, yo, k16, yo, k5, yo, k6, yo, k16, yo, k4.
9th row K5, yo, k16, yo, [k7, yo] twice, k16, yo, k5.
11th row K22, yo, k8, yo, k9, yo, k22. 64 sts.
12th row Rep 2nd row.
K 12 rows.
Shape instep
Next row K36, skp, turn.
Next row Sl 1, p8, p2tog, turn.
Next row Sl 1, k8, skp, turn.
Rep the last 2 rows 5 times more, then work first of the 2 rows again.
Next row Sl 1, k to end.
Next row K19, k2tog, k8, skp, k19. 48 sts.
Next row K9, leave these sts on a holder, bind off one st, [slip the st now on right-hand needle back onto left-hand needle, cast on 2 sts onto left-hand needle, bind off 4 sts] 14 times, slip the st back onto left-hand needle, cast on 2 sts onto left-hand needle, bind off 3 sts, k to end, leave these 9 sts on a holder.
Sew sole and back heel seam.
With wrong side facing and size 2 needles, k across 18 sts on holder for ankle strap.**
Next row Cast on 4 sts at beg of row, k to end, cast on 22 sts and turn.
Buttonhole row K1, skp, yo, k to end.
K 2 rows.
Bind off.
Sew on button.

left bootie

Work as given for Right Bootie to **.
Next row Cast on 22 sts at beg of row, k to end, cast on 4 sts and turn.
Buttonhole row K to last 3 sts, yo, k2tog, k1.
K 2 rows.
Bind off.
Sew on button.

size
To fit age 3–6 months

materials
1 x 1^3/$_4$oz/50g ball Debbie Bliss Baby Cashmerino in teal
Pair of size 2 knitting needles

gauge
28 sts and 50 rows to 4in square over garter st using size 2 needles.

abbreviations
See page 25.

baby boots

to make

With size 2 needles, cast on 18 sts (for first half of cuff) and k 12 rows.
Break off yarn and leave these sts on a holder.
With size 2 needles, cast on 18 sts (for second half of cuff) and k 12 rows.
Join cuff halves
Next row [K1, p1] 9 times, then [k1, p1] 9 times across first half of cuff on holder. 36 sts.
Next row [K1, p1] to end.
Rep the last row 6 times more.
Shape instep
Next row (RS) K33, turn.
Next row K10, turn.
Work 24 rows in garter st on center 10 sts.
Next row K1, skp, k4, k2tog, k1. 8 sts.
K 1 row.
Break off yarn.
With RS facing, rejoin yarn at base of instep, pick up and k 13 sts evenly along side of instep, k across center 8 sts, then pick up and k 13 sts evenly along other side of instep, k rem 13 sts. 60 sts.
K 13 rows.
Beg with a k row, work 7 rows in St st.
Next row [P next st tog with corresponding st 7 rows below] to end.
Break off yarn.
Shape sole
Next row Slip first 25 sts onto right-hand needle, rejoin yarn and k 10 sts, turn.
Next row K9, k2tog, turn.
Rep last row until 20 sts rem.
Bind off.

to finish

Sew back seam. With back seam at center of bind-off, sew heel seam.

measurements
Approximately $35^1/_2$in x $43^1/_4$in

materials
15 x $1^3/_4$oz/50g balls Debbie Bliss Baby Cashmerino in ecru (M)
Small amount of contrasting yarn (C) for embroidery
Sizes 2 and 3 circular knitting needles
Cable needle

gauge
25 sts and 34 rows to 4in square over St st using size 3 needles.

sampler blanket

abbreviations

C4B = slip next 2 sts onto cable needle and hold at back of work, k2, then k2 from cable needle.

C4F = slip next 2 sts onto cable needle and hold at front of work, k2, then k2 from cable needle.

C5F = slip next 3 sts onto cable needle and hold at front of work, k2, then slip the p st from cable needle back onto left-hand needle, p this st, then k2 from cable needle.

C6B = slip next 3 sts onto cable needle and hold at back of work, k3, then k3 from cable needle.

C6F = slip next 3 sts onto cable needle and hold at front of work, k3, then k3 from cable needle.

C3BP = slip next st onto cable needle and hold at back of work, k2, then p1 from cable needle.

C3FP = slip next 2 sts onto cable needle and hold at front of work, p1, then k2 from cable needle.

C4BP = slip next 2 sts onto cable needle and hold at back of work, k2, then p2 from cable needle.

C4FP = slip next 2 sts onto cable needle and hold at front of work, p2, then k2 from cable needle.

C5BP = slip next 2 sts onto cable needle and hold at back of work, k3, then p2 from cable needle.

C5FP = slip next 3 sts onto cable needle and hold at front of work, p2, then k3 from cable needle.

T5L = slip next 2 sts onto cable needle and hold at front of work, k2, p1, then k2 from cable needle.

MB = k into front, back, and front of next st, [turn and k3] 3 times, turn and sl 1, k2tog, psso.

Also see page 25.

motif A
(worked over 40 sts)

1st row (right side) P9, T5L, p12, T5L, p9.
2nd row K9, p2, k1, p2, k12, p2, k1, p2, k9.
3rd row P8, C3BP, k1, C3FP, p10, C3BP, k1, C3FP, p8.
4th row K8, p2, k1, p1, k1, p2, k10, p2, k1, p1, k1, p2, k8.
5th row P7, C3BP, k1, p1, k1, C3FP, p8, C3BP, k1, p1, k1, C3FP, p7.
6th row K7, p2, [k1, p1] twice, k1, p2, k8, p2, [k1, p1] twice, k1, p2, k7.
7th row P6, C3BP, [k1, p1] twice, k1, C3FP, p6, C3BP, [k1, p1] twice, k1, C3FP, p6.
8th row K6, p2, [k1, p1] 3 times, k1, p2, k6, p2, [k1, p1] 3 times, k1, p2, k6.
9th row P5, C3BP, [k1, p1] 3 times, k1, C3FP, p4, C3BP, [k1, p1] 3 times, k1, C3FP, p5.
10th row K5, p2, [k1, p1] 4 times, k1, p2, k4, p2, [k1, p1] 4 times, k1, p2, k5.
11th row P4, C3BP, [k1, p1] 4 times, k1, C3FP, p2, C3BP, [k1, p1] 4 times, k1, C3FP, p4.
12th row K4, p2, [k1, p1] 5 times, k1, p2, k2, p2, [k1, p1] 5 times, k1, p2, k4.
13th–36th rows Rep 1st–12th rows twice more.
37th row P4, k3, [p1, k1] 4 times, p1, k3, p2, k3, [p1, k1] 4 times, p1, k3, p4.
38th row K4, p3, [k1, p1] 4 times, k1, p3, k2, p3, [k1, p1] 4 times, k1, p3, k4.

motif B
(worked over 40 sts)

1st row (right side) P9, C3BP, p5, C6B, p5, C3FP, p9.
2nd row K9, p2, k6, p6, k6, p2, k9.
3rd row P8, C3BP, p4, C5BP, C5FP, p4, C3FP, p8.
4th row K8, p2, k5, p3, k4, p3, k5, p2, k8.
5th row P7, C3BP, p3, C5BP, p4, C5FP, p3, C3FP, p7.
6th row K7, p2, k1, MB, k2, p3, k8, p3, k2, MB, k1, p2, k7.
7th row P7, C3FP, p3, k3, p8, k3, p3, C3BP, p7.
8th row K8, p2, k3, p3, k8, p3, k3, p2, k8.

9th row P8, C3FP, p2, C5FP, p4, C5BP, p2, C3BP, p8.

10th row K9, p2, [k4, p3] twice, k4, p2, k9.

11th row P9, C3FP, p3, C5FP, C5BP, p3, C3BP, p9.

12th row K8, MB, k1, p2, k5, p6, k5, p2, k1, MB, k8.

13th–38th rows Rep 1st–12th twice more, then 1st and 2nd rows again.

motif C
(worked over 40 sts)

1st row (right side) P10, C5F, p10, C5F, p10.

2nd row K10, p2, k1, p2, k10, p2, k1, p2, k10.

3rd row P9, C3BP, k1, C3FP, p8, C3BP, k1, C3FP, p9.

4th row K9, p2, k1, p1, k1, p2, k8, p2, k1, p1, k1, p2, k9.

5th row P8, C3BP, k1, p1, k1, C3FP, p6, C3BP, k1, p1, k1, C3FP, p8.

6th row K8, p2, [k1, p1] twice, k1, p2, k6, p2, [k1, p1] twice, k1, p2, k8.

7th row P7, C3BP, [k1, p1] twice, k1, C3FP, p4, C3BP, [k1, p1] twice, k1, C3FP, p7.

8th row K7, p2, [k1, p1] 3 times, k1, p2, k4, p2, [k1, p1] 3 times, k1, p2, k7.

9th row P6, C3BP, [k1, p1] 3 times, k1, C3FP, p2, C3BP, [k1, p1] 3 times, k1, C3FP, p6.

10th row K6, p2, [k1, p1] 4 times, k1, p2, k2, p2, [k1, p1] 4 times, k1, p2, k6.

11th row P6, C3FP, [p1, k1] 3 times, p1, C3BP, p2, C3FP, [p1, k1] 3 times, p1, C3BP, p6.

12th row Rep 8th row.

13th row P7, C3FP, [p1, k1] twice, p1, C3BP, p4, C3FP, [p1, k1] twice, p1, C3BP, p7.

14th row Rep 6th row.

15th row P8, C3FP, p1, k1, p1, C3BP, p6, C3FP, p1, k1, p1, C3BP, p8.

16th row Rep 4th row.

17th row P9, C3FP, p1, C3BP, p8, C3FP, p1, C3BP, p9.

18th row Rep 2nd row.

19th–38th rows Rep 1st–18th rows once more then 1st and 2nd rows again.

motif D
(worked over 40 sts)

1st row P8, k2, p8, C4B, p8, k2, p8.

2nd row K8, p2, k8, p4, k8, p2, k8.

3rd row P8, C4FP, p4, C4BP, C4FP, p4, C4BP, p8.

4th row K10, [p2, k4] 3 times, p2, k10.

5th row P10, C4FP, C4BP, p4, C4FP, C4BP, p10.

6th row K12, p4, k8, p4, k12.

7th row P12, C4B, p4, MB, p3, C4F, p12.

8th row Rep 6th row.

9th row P10, C4BP, C4FP, p4, C4BP, C4FP, p10.

10th row Rep 4th row.

11th row P8, C4BP, p4, C4FP, C4BP, p4, C4FP, p8.

12th row Rep 2nd row.

13th row P8, k2, p4, MB, p3, C4B, p4, MB, p3, k2, p8.

14th row K8, p2, k8, p4, k8, p2, k8.

15th–26th rows Rep 3rd–14th rows once more.

27th–36th rows Rep 3rd–12th rows.

37th and 38th rows Rep 1st and 2nd rows.

to make

With size 2 circular needle and M, cast on 240 sts.
K 19 rows.
1st row K10, [p1, k1] to last 12 sts, p1, k11.
2nd row K11, [p1, k1] to last 11 sts, p1, k10.
Rep the last 2 rows 3 times more.
Change to size 3 circular needle.
First row of motifs
1st row (right side) K10, seed st 5, [p38, seed st 5] to last 53 sts, k38, seed st 5, k10.
2nd row K10, seed st 5, p38, seed st 5, [k38, seed st 5] to last 10 sts, k10.
3rd row Rep 1st row.
4th row (inc row) (wrong side) K10, seed st 5, p38, seed st 5, k18, M1, k2, M1, k18, seed st 5, k11, M1, k16, M1, k11, seed st, 5, k18, M1, k2, M1, k18, seed st 5, k10, M1, k18, M1, k10, seed st 5, k10. 248 sts.
5th row K10, seed st 5, work across 1st row of motif A, seed st 5, work across 1st row of motif D, seed st 5, work across 1st row of motif C, seed st 5, work across 1st row of motif B, seed st 5, k38, seed st 5, k10.
6th row K10, seed st 5, p38, seed st 5, work across 2nd row of motif B, seed st 5, work across 2nd row of motif C, seed st 5, work across 2nd row of motif D, seed st 5, work across 2nd row of motif A, seed st 5, k10.
The last 2 rows set the position of the motifs with seed st between and garter st edging.
Working correct patt rows, work 36 rows more.
43rd row (dec row) K10, seed st 5, p9, p2tog, p18, p2tog, p9, seed st 5, p18, [p2tog] twice, p18, seed st 5, p10, p2tog, p16, p2tog, p10, seed st 5, p18, [p2tog] twice, p18, seed st 5, k38, seed st 5, k10. 240 sts.
44th row K10, seed st 5, p38, seed st 5, [k38, seed st 5] to last 10 sts, k10.
45th and 46th rows Rep 1st and 2nd rows.
Change to size 2 circular needle.
1st row K10, [p1, k1] to last 12 sts, p1, k11.
2nd row K11, [p1, k1] to last 11 sts, p1, k10.
Rep the last 2 rows 3 times more.
Change to size 3 circular needle.
**Second row of motifs
1st row (right side) K10, seed st 5, [p38, seed st 5] to last 10 sts, k10.
2nd row K10, seed st 5, [k38, seed st 5] to last 10 sts, k10.
3rd row Rep 1st row.
4th row (inc row) (wrong side) K10, seed st 5, k18, M1, k2, M1, k18, seed st 5, k11, M1, k16, M1, k11, seed st 5, k18, M1, k2, M1, k18, seed st 5, k10, M1, k18, M1, k10, seed st 5, k18, M1, k2, M1, k18, seed st 5, k10. 250 sts.
5th row K10, seed st 5, work across 1st row of motif B, seed st 5, work across 1st row of motif A, seed st 5, work across 1st row of motif D, seed st 5, work across 1st row of motif C, seed st 5, work across 1st row of motif B, seed st 5, k10.
6th row K10, seed st 5, work across 2nd row of motif B, seed st 5, work across 2nd row of motif C, seed st 5, work across 2nd row of motif D, seed st 5, work across 2nd row of motif A, seed st 5, work across 2nd row of motif B, seed st 5, k10.
The last 2 rows set the position of the motifs with seed st between and garter st edging.

Working correct patt rows, work 36 rows more.

43rd row (dec row) K10, seed st 5, p18, [p2tog] twice, p18, seed st 5, p9, p2tog, p18, p2tog, p9, seed st 5, p18, [p2tog] twice, p18, seed st 5, p10, p2tog, p16, p2tog, p10, seed st 5, p18, [p2tog] twice, p18, seed st 5, k10. 240 sts.

44th row K10, seed st 5, [k38, seed st 5] to last 10 sts, k10.

45th and 46th rows Rep 1st and 2nd rows.

Change to size 2 circular needle.

1st row K10, [p1, k1] to last 12 sts, p1, k11.

2nd row K11, [p1, k1] to last 11 sts, p1, k10.

Rep the last 2 rows 3 times more.

Change to size 3 circular needle.

Third row of motifs

1st row (right side) K10, seed st 5, [p38, seed st 5] to last 10 sts, k10.

2nd row K10, seed st 5, [k38, seed st 5] to last 10 sts, k10.

3rd row Rep 1st row.

4th row (inc row) (wrong side) K10, seed st 5, k11, M1, k16, M1, k11, seed st, 5, k18, M1, k2, M1, k18, seed st 5, k10, M1, k18, M1, k10, seed st 5, k18, M1, k2, M1, k18, seed st 5, k11, M1, k16, M1, k11, seed st 5, k10. 250 sts.

5th row K10, seed st 5, work across 1st row of motif C, seed st 5, work across 1st row of motif B, seed st 5, work across 1st row of motif A, seed st 5, work across 1st row of motif D, seed st 5, work across 1st row of motif C, seed st 5, k10.

6th row K10, seed st 5, work across 2nd row of motif C, seed st 5, work across 2nd row of motif D, seed st 5, work across 2nd row of motif A, seed st 5, work across 2nd row of motif B, seed st 5, work across 2nd row of motif C, seed st 5, k10.

These 2 rows set the position of the motifs with seed st between and garter st edging.

Working correct patt rows, work 36 rows more.

43rd row (dec row) K10, seed st 5, p10, p2tog, p16, p2tog, p10, seed st 5, p18, [p2tog] twice, p18, seed st 5, p9, p2tog, p18, p2tog, p9, seed st 5, p18, [p2tog] twice, p18, seed st 5, p10, p2tog, p16, p2tog, p10, seed st 5, k10. 240 sts.

44th row K10, seed st 5, [k38, seed st 5] to last 10 sts, k10.

45th and 46th rows Rep 1st and 2nd rows.

Change to size 2 circular needle.

1st row K10, [p1, k1] to last 12 sts, p1, k11.

2nd row K11, [p1, k1] to last 11 sts, p1, k10.

Rep the last 2 rows 3 times more.**

Change to size 3 circular needle.

Fourth row of motifs

1st row (right side) K10, seed st 5, [p38, seed st 5] to last 10 sts, k10.

2nd row K10, seed st 5, [k38, seed st 5] to last 10 sts, k10.

3rd row Rep 1st row.

4th row (inc row) (wrong side) K10, seed st, 5, k18, M1, k2, M1, k18, seed st 5, k10, M1, k18, M1, k10, seed st 5, k18, M1, k2, M1, k18, seed st 5, k11, M1, k16, M1, k11, seed st 5, k18, M1, k2, M1, k18, seed st 5, k10. 250 sts

5th row K10, work across 1st row of motif D, seed st 5, work across 1st row of motif C, seed st 5,

work across 1st row of motif B, seed st 5, work across 1st row of motif A, seed st 5, work across 1st row of motif D, seed st 5, k10.

6th row K10, seed st 5, work across 2nd row of motif D, seed st 5, work across 2nd row of motif A, seed st 5, work across 2nd row of motif B, seed st 5, work across 2nd row of motif C, seed st 5, work across 2nd row of motif D, seed st 5, k10.

The last 2 rows set the position of the motifs with seed st between and garter st edging.

Working correct patt rows, work 36 rows more.

43rd row (dec row) K10, seed st 5, p18, [p2tog] twice, p18, seed st 5, p10, p2tog, p16, p2tog, p10, seed st 5, p18, [p2tog] twice, p18, seed st 5, p9, p2tog, p18, p2tog, p9, seed st 5, p18, [p2tog] twice, p18, seed st 5, k10. 240 sts.

44th row K10, seed st 5, [k38, seed st 5] to last 10 sts, k10.

45th and 46th rows Rep 1st and 2nd rows.

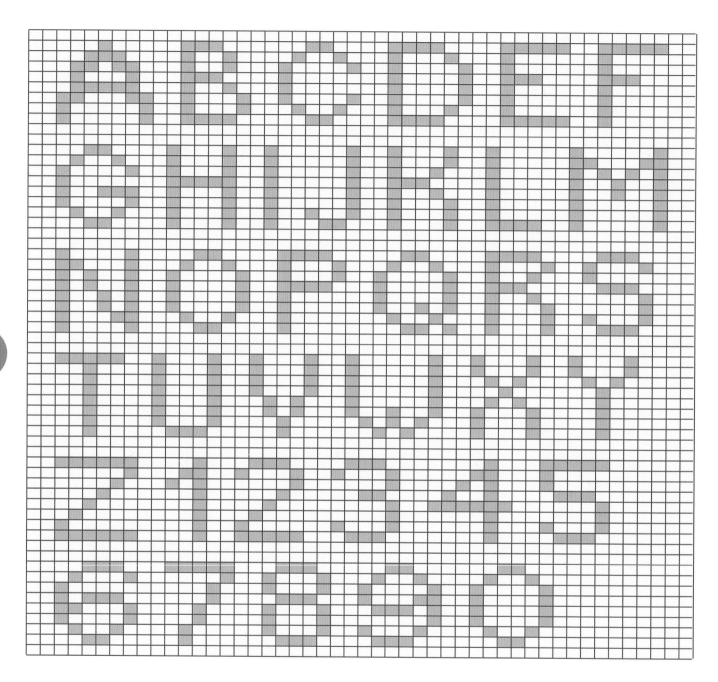

Change to size 2 circular needle.

1st row K10, [p1, k1] to last 12 sts, p1, k11.

2nd row K11, [p1, k1] to last 11 sts, p1, k10.

Rep the last 2 rows 3 times more.

Change to size 3 circular needle.

Fifth row of motifs

1st row (right side) K10, seed st 5, [p38, seed st 5] to last 10 sts, k10.

2nd row K10, seed st 5, [k38, seed st 5] to last 10 sts, k10.

3rd row Rep 1st row.

4th row (inc row) (wrong side) K10, seed st 5, k10, M1, k18, M1, k10, seed st 5, k18, M1, k2, M1, k18, seed st 5, k11, M1, k16, M1, k11, seed st 5, k18, M1, k2, M1, k18, seed st 5, k10, M1, k18, M1, k10, seed st 5, k10. 250 sts.

5th row K10, seed st 5, work across 1st row of motif A, seed st 5, work across 1st row of motif D, seed st 5, work across 1st row of motif C, seed st 5, work across 1st row of motif B, seed st 5, work across 1st row of motif A, seed st 5, k10.

6th row K10, seed st 5, work across 2nd row of motif A, seed st 5, work across 2nd row of motif B, seed st 5, work across 2nd row of motif C, seed st 5, work across 2nd row of motif D, seed st 5, work across 2nd row of motif A, seed st 5, k10.

The last 2 rows set the position of the motifs with seed st between and garter st edging.

Working correct patt rows, work 36 rows more.

43rd row (dec row) K10, seed st 5, p9, p2tog, p18, p2tog, p9, seed st 5, p18, [p2tog] twice, p18, seed st 5, p10, p2tog, p16, p2tog, p10, seed st 5, p18, [p2tog] twice, p18, seed st 5, p9, p2tog, p18, p2tog, p9, seed st 5, k10. 240 sts.

44th row K10, seed st 5, [k38, seed st 5] to last 10 sts, k10.

45th and 46th rows Rep 1st and 2nd rows.

Change to size 2 circular needle.

1st row K10, [p1, k1] to last 12 sts, p1, k11.

2nd row K11, [p1, k1] to last 11 sts, p1, k10.

Rep the last 2 rows 3 times more.

Change to size 3 circular needle.

Sixth and seventh rows of motifs

Work as Second and Third row of motifs from ** to **.

K 19 rows.

Bind off.

embroidery

Using your own selection of letters and numbers from the Chart opposite and contrasting yarn (C), duplicate stitch the initials and date onto the blank square at the lower left-hand corner.

measurements
Approximately 3½in tall

materials
1 x 1¾oz/50g ball Debbie Bliss Baby Cashmerino in gray (A)
Small amount of Debbie Bliss Cashmerino Aran in each of charcoal (B) and gold (C)
Pair each of sizes 2 and 6 knitting needles

gague
29 sts and 42 rows to 4in square over St st using size 2 needles.

abbreviations
sk2p = slip 1, k2tog, pass slipped st over.
Also see page 25.

body

With size 2 needles and A, cast on 26 sts.
Beg with a k row, work in St st until piece measures 7in, ending with a k row.
Bind off.

beak

With size 6 needles and C, cast on 6 sts.
Next 2 rows K4, turn, sl 1, k3.
Next 2 rows K5, turn, sl 1, k4.
Next 2 rows K to end.
Next 2 rows K5, turn, sl 1, k4.
Next 2 rows K4, turn, sl 1, k3.
Bind off knitwise.
Sew together cast-on and bound-off edges.

feet (make 2)

With size 6 needles and B, cast on 13 sts.
1st and all wrong side rows K.
2nd row K5, sk2p, k5.
4th row K4, sk2p, k4.
6th row K3, sk2p, k3.
Bind off rem 7 sts.

to finish

Sew together cast-on and bound-off edges of body to form a tube. Fold the tube flat with the seam at one side and sew together from the seam to the fold. On the open edge, place a marker on the fold. Refold and match the cast-on/bound-off seam to the fold marker and sew the open edges together, leaving a gap large enough to insert stuffing. Stuff and sew up gap in seam. Position beak on bird and sew in place firmly. Position feet on bird and sew in place securely. With B, sew a few sts to form eyes.

little bird **toy**

big bird cushion

measurements
Approximately 33½in tall

materials
19 x 1¾oz/50g balls of Debbie Bliss Rialto Aran in charcoal (A)
1 x 1¾oz/50g ball of Debbie Bliss Cashmerino Aran in each of mid gray (B) and yellow (C)
Size 8 circular knitting needle
Pair each of sizes 6 and 7 needles
36½in x 61½in fabric for lining
Polystyrene beads
Batting for beak and feet
Scraps of black felt for eyes

gauge
18 sts and 24 rows to 4in square over St st using size 8 needles.

abbreviations

sk2p = slip 1, k2tog, pass slipped st over.
Also see page 25.

note

The knitted piece is slightly smaller than the inner lining to prevent sagging.

to make

With size 8 circular needle and A, cast on 156 sts.
Beg with a k row, work in St st until piece measures 59in.
Bind off.

beak

With size 6 needles and C, cast on 27 sts.
K 15 rows.
Next row (right side) K6, sk2p, k6. K 5 rows.
Next row K5, sk2p, k5. K 5 rows.
Next row K4, sk2p, k4. K 6 rows.
Bind off knitwise.

feet (make 4)

With size 7 needles and B, cast on 61 sts.
1st and all wrong side rows K.
2nd row K29, sk2p, k29.
4th row K28, sk2p, k28.
6th row K27, sk2p, k27.
Cont in this way, decreasing 2 sts on every right-side row until 23 sts rem, ending with a right-side row. Bind off knitwise.

to make lining

Cut a piece of fabric 36½in x 61½in. With right sides together and taking ⅝in seams throughout, sew the short sides of fabric piece together to form a tube (this seam forms the base of the bird). Fold the tube flat with the seam at one side and sew together from the seam to the fold (this forms the back of the bird). Open out the unstitched side and refold the fabric so the first seam lies centrally, and stitch the seam, leaving 2in unstitched at one end. Turn right-side out and fill with polystyrene beads. Stitch the opening closed.

to finish

Sew together cast-on and bound-off edges of knitted piece to form a tube (this seam forms the base of the bird). Fold the tube flat with the seam at one side and sew together from the seam to the fold (this seam forms the back of the bird). On the open edge, place a marker on the fold. Open out the unstitched side and insert the filled lining; then matching the first seam (base) to the marker, stitch the seam closed so that the first seam lies centrally. Sew together row ends of beak, then fold beak in half with seam at center of bound-off edge and sew together to form end of beak. Cut pieces of batting and place inside beak, then securely sew to the front of the bird. Using one of the feet as a template, cut pieces of batting slightly smaller than knitted foot. Sew the feet together in pairs with the batting in the center. Position the feet on the bird and stitch in place. Cut two ¾in circles of felt for eyes and stitch in place.

fair isle hangers

measurements
To fit a 8³/₄in plain wooden hanger

materials
1 x 1³/₄oz/50g ball (or small amount) Debbie Bliss Baby Cashmerino in each of pale pink, lime, teal, duck egg, ecru, red, and pink
Pair of size 3 knitting needles
8³/₄in plain wooden hanger
Polyester batting
12in of narrow ribbon

gauge
25 sts and 34 rows to 4in over Fair Isle St st using size 3 needles.

abbreviations
See page 25.

note
You may find it difficult to obtain a 8³/₄in wooden hanger, but you can easily cut down a standard-width hanger to the right size using a saw. If you want to cover a hanger of a different width, you will need to recalculate the number of sts. The pattern is worked over a multiple of 8 sts, plus 1 edge st.

to make
With size 3 needles and main color from your chosen chart, cast on 57 sts.
Beg with a k row, work 2 rows in St st.
Now cont in St st and work from chart as follows:
1st chart row (right side) K 1 edge st, [k8 patt rep sts] 7 times.
2nd chart row [P 8 patt rep sts] 7 times, p 1 edge st.
These 2 rows set the position of the chart and are repeated.
Cont until all 15 chart rows have been worked, then rep these 15 rows once more.
Bind off.

to finish
Pad a hanger with batting and stitch in place. Fold knitting in half aligning cast-on and bound-off edges and sew side seams from fold to edge. Find the center of the cover and thread the hanger hook through the knitting at this point. Ease the cover over the hanger and sew together cast-on to bound-off edges. Tie a ribbon around the base of the hook.

	pale pink		lime		teal		duck egg		ecru		red		pink

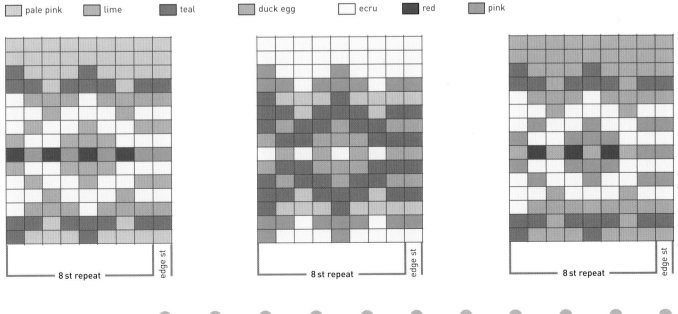

8 st repeat — edge st

8 st repeat — edge st

8 st repeat — edge st

measurements
Approximately 10 (16½)in tall

materials
Little bear 2 x 1¾oz/50g balls Debbie Bliss Baby Cashmerino in stone (A)
Pair of size 2 knitting needles
Big bear 4 x 1¾oz/50g balls Debbie Bliss Cashmerino Chunky in stone (B)
Pair of size 8 knitting needles
Small amount of chocolate yarn for embroidery
1yd of ⅝in wide ribbon for each bear
Washable toy stuffing (see Safety Note on page 47)
Scraps of chocolate felt and matching sewing thread

gauge
28 sts and 58 rows in Baby Cashmerino (A) using size 2 needles and 18 sts and 38 rows in
Cashmerino Chunky (B) using size 8 needles, both to 4in square over garter st.

big & little bear

abbreviations
See page 25.

notes
Both bears are worked in garter stitch (k every row).
Little bear is made using Baby Cashmerino and size 2 knitting needles throughout.
Big bear is made using Cashmerino Chunky and size 8 needles throughout.
All the instructions are for both bears, different needles and yarns create the size difference.

body

The body is worked starting at the neck edge.
With size 2 (size 8) needles and A (B), cast on 12 sts and k 1 row.
Shape shoulders
Next row Cast on 2 sts at beg of row, k to end.
Rep this row 3 times more. 20 sts. K 4 rows.
Next row K1, M1, k to last st, M1, k1. 22 sts. K 5 rows.**
Rep the last 6 rows 5 times more. 32 sts.
Shape base
Next row K1, [ssk, k11, k2tog] twice, k1. 28 sts. K 1 row.
Next row K1, [ssk, k9, k2tog] twice, k1. 24 sts. K 1 row.
***Next row** K1, [ssk, k7, k2tog] twice, k1. 20 sts. K 1 row.
Cont to dec 4 sts in this way on every alt row until 8 sts rem.
Next row K1, sl 1, k2tog, psso, k3tog, k1. 4 sts.
Next row [K2tog] twice. 2 sts.
Next row K2tog and finish off.

body front

Work as Body Back to **.
Next row K1, M1, k to last st, M1, k1. 24 sts. K 5 rows.
Next row K1, M1, k10, M1, k2, M1, k10, M1, k1. 28 sts. K 5 rows.
Next row K1, M1, k10, M1, k6, M1, k10, M1, k1. 32 sts. K 5 rows.
Next row K1, M1, k to last st, M1, k1. 34 sts. K 5 rows.
Rep the last 6 rows once more. 36 sts.
Next row K1, ssk, k6, ssk, k5, k2tog, ssk, k5, k2tog, k6, k2tog, k1. 30 sts. K 1 row.
Next row K1, ssk, k5, ssk, k3, k2tog, ssk, k3, k2tog, k5, k2tog, k1. 24 sts. K 1 row.
Now work as Body Back from *** to end.

head

With size 2 (size 8) needles and A (B), cast on 4 sts.
1st row K.
2nd row K1, [M1, k1] to end. 7 sts.
Rep the last 2 rows once more. 13 sts.
5th, 7th, 9th, and 11th rows K.
6th row [K1, M1, k5, M1] twice, k1. 17 sts.
8th row K1, M1, k6, M1, k3, M1, k6, M1, k1. 21 sts.
10th row K1, M1, k7, M1, k5, M1, k7, M1, k1. 25 sts.
12th row K1, M1, k8, M1, k7, M1, k8, M1, k1. 29 sts. K 2 rows.
15th row K2, [ssk, k1] 3 times, k8, [k2tog, k1] 3 times, k1. 23 sts.
16th row K4, M1, k3, M1, k9, M1, k3, M1, k4. 27 sts. K 3 rows.
20th row [K4, M1] twice, k11, [M1, k4] twice. 31 sts. K 3 rows.
24th row K4, M1, k5, M1, k13, M1, k5, M1, k4. 35 sts. K 1 row.
26th row K4, M1, k6, M1, k15, M1, k6, M1, k4. 39 sts. K 1 row.
28th row K4, M1, k7, M1, k17, M1, k7, M1, k4. 43 sts. K 1 row.
30th row K3, [M1, k4] 3 times, M1, k13, M1, [k4, M1] 3 times, k3. 51 sts. K 12 rows.
43rd row K9, k2tog, [k8, k2tog] 4 times. 46 sts. K 1 row.
45th row K8, k2tog, [k7, k2tog] 4 times. 41 sts. K 1 row.
47th row K7, k2tog, [k6, k2tog] 4 times. 36 sts. K 1 row.
Dec 5 sts in this way on next row and 4 foll alt rows. 11 sts. K 1 row.
Next row Sl 1, k2tog, psso, [k2tog] 4 times. 5 sts.
Break off yarn, thread through rem sts, pull together, and secure.
Sew seam, leaving a gap. Stuff carefully and sew up gap in seam.

ears (make 2)

With size 2 (size 8) needles and A (B), cast on 11 sts. K 3 rows.
4th row K1, ssk, k5, k2tog, k1. K 1 row.
6th row K1, ssk, k3, k2tog, k1. K 1 row.
8th row K1, ssk, k1, k2tog, k1. 5 sts. K 1 row.
10th row K1, M1, k3, M1, k1. K 1 row.
12th row K1, M1, k5, M1, k1. K 1 row.
14th row K1, M1, k7, M1, k1. 11 sts. K 2 rows.
Bind off.
Fold in half and slip stitch around edge.

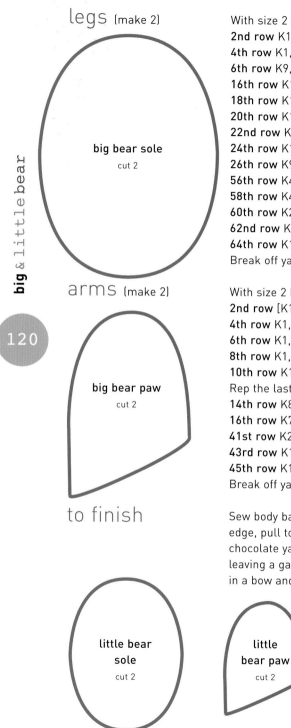

legs (make 2)

big bear sole
cut 2

arms (make 2)

big bear paw
cut 2

to finish

little bear
sole
cut 2

little
bear paw
cut 2

With size 2 (size 8) needles and A (B), cast on 15 sts. K 1 row.
2nd row K1, M1, k4, M1, k1, M1, k3, M1, k1, M1, k4, M1, k1. 21 sts. K 1 row.
4th row K1, M1, k6, M1, k2, M1, k3, M1, k2, M1, k6, M1, k1. 27 sts. K 1 row.
6th row K9, M1, k3, [M1, k1] 3 times, M1, k3, M1, k9. 33 sts. K 9 rows.
16th row K12, ssk, k5, k2tog, k12. 31 sts. K 1 row.
18th row K12, ssk, k3, k2tog, k12. 29 sts. K 1 row.
20th row K12, ssk, k1, k2tog, k12. 27 sts. K 1 row.
22nd row K11, ssk, k1, k2tog, k11. 25 sts. K 1 row.
24th row K10, ssk, k1, k2tog, k10. 23 sts. K 1 row.
26th row K9, ssk, k1, k2tog, k9. 21 sts. K 28 rows.
56th row K4, ssk, k9, k2tog, k4. 19 sts. K 1 row.
58th row K4, ssk, k7, k2tog, k4. 17 sts. K 1 row.
60th row K2, ssk, k2tog, k5, ssk, k2tog, k2. 13 sts. K 1 row.
62nd row K1, ssk, k2tog, sl 2tog, k1, pass 2 slipped sts over, ssk, k2tog, k1. 7 sts. K 1 row.
64th row K1, ssk, k1, k2tog, k1. 5 sts.
Break off yarn, thread through rem sts, pull together, and secure.

With size 2 (size 8) needles and A (B), cast on 7 sts. K 1 row.
2nd row [K1, M1, k2, M1] twice, k1. 11 sts. K 1 row.
4th row K1, M1, [k3, M1] 3 times, k1. 15 sts. K 1 row.
6th row K1, M1, k4, M1, k5, M1, k4, M1, k1. 19 sts. K 1 row.
8th row K1, M1, k17, M1, k1. 21 sts. K 1 row.
10th row K1, M1, k7, ssk, k1, k2tog, k7, M1, k1. 21 sts. K 1 row.
Rep the last 2 rows once more.
14th row K8, ssk, k1, k2tog, k8. 19 sts. K 1 row.
16th row K7, ssk, k1, k2tog, k7. 17 sts. K 24 rows.
41st row K2, ssk, k2tog, k5, ssk, k2tog, k2. 13 sts. K 1 row.
43rd row K1, ssk, k2tog, sl 2tog, k1, pass 2 slipped sts over, ssk, k2tog, k1. 7 sts. K 1 row.
45th row K1, ssk, k1, k2tog, k1. 5 sts.
Break off yarn, thread through rem sts, pull together, and secure.

Sew body back to body front leaving neck edge open. Stuff firmly and run a thread around neck edge, pull together slightly, and secure. Sew ears to head. Embroider facial features with chocolate yarn. Sew head to body at neck. Fold each arm and each leg in half and sew seam, leaving a gap. Stuff arms and legs firmly, sew up gaps, and sew to body. Tie ribbon around neck in a bow and trim ends. Using the templates, cut paw and foot pads from felt and sew in place.

122 memory book cover

measurements
To fit a 6^1/$_4$in x 8^1/$_4$in notebook

materials
2 x 1^3/$_4$oz/50g balls Debbie Bliss Baby Cashmerino in silver (A), 1 x 1^3/$_4$oz/50g ball in ecru (B), and small amount in pale pink (C)
Pair of size 3 knitting needles
Small amount of chocolate six-strand cotton embroidery floss
4 small mother-of-pearl buttons (optional)
6^1/$_4$in x 8^1/$_4$in notebook

gauge
25 sts and 34 rows to 4in square over St st using size 3 needles.

abbreviations
See page 25.

note
The memory book cover is worked sideways starting at the inside back cover.

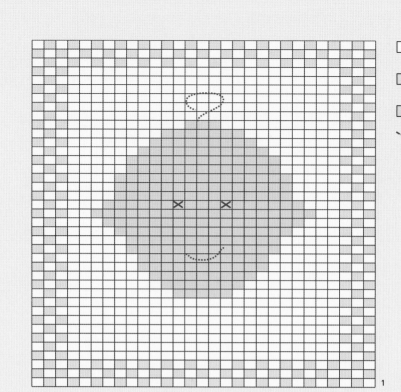

| | With B, k on right-side rows, p on wrong-side rows |
| With B, p on right-side rows, k on wrong-side rows |
| With C, k on right-side rows, p on wrong-side rows |
| Embroider on completion |

124

pattern A

1st row (right side) [K1, p1] twice, k to last 4 sts, [p1, k1] twice.
2nd row K1, [p1, k1] twice, p to last 5 sts, [k1, p1] twice, k1.
These 2 rows form St st with seed st edges and are repeated.

cover

With size 3 needles and A, cast on 55 sts.
Seed st row (right side) K1, [p1, k1] to end.
Rep this row 3 times more.
Work 21 rows in patt A, so ending with a 1st row.
Next row (fold-line row) (wrong side) K1, p1, k to last 2 sts, p1, k1.
Work 6 rows in seed st.
Work 45 rows in patt A, so ending with a 1st row.
Work 21 rows in seed st.
Work 45 rows in patt A, so ending with a 1st row.
Work 6 rows in seed st.
Next row (fold-line row) (wrong side) K1, p1, k to last 2 sts, p1, k1.
Work 21 rows in patt A, so ending with a 1st row.
Next row K1, [p1, k1] to end.
Work 4 rows in seed st.
Bind off in seed st.

front patch

With size 3 needles and B, cast on 29 sts.
Beg with a right-side row, work 39 rows in patt from Chart.
Bind off in seed st.
Embroider features using 3 strands of embroidery floss.

to finish

Stitch patch to front cover and decorate with a small button in each corner. Fold cover along
fold-line rows and stitch inside cover flaps to outside cover along edges.

128 striped cardigan

sizes and measurements
To fit ages 3–6 (6–9: 9–12: 12–18: 18–24) months
finished measurements
Chest 20 (22: 23^1/$_2$: 25^1/$_2$: 27^1/$_2$)in
Length to shoulder 9^1/$_2$ (10^1/$_4$: 11: 12^1/$_2$: 14^1/$_4$)in
Sleeve length 6 (6^3/$_4$: 7^1/$_2$: 8^1/$_2$: 9^1/$_2$)in

materials
2 (2: 2: 3: 3) x 1^3/$_4$oz/50g balls Debbie Bliss Baby Cashmerino in each of gray (M) and ecru (C)
Pair each of sizes 2 and 3 knitting needles
Size 2 circular knitting needle
6 (6: 6: 7: 7) buttons

gauge
25 sts and 34 rows to 4in square over St st using size 3 needles.

abbreviations
See page 25.

back

With size 2 needles and C, cast on 65 (71: 77: 83: 89) sts.
1st rib row K1, [p1, k1] to end.
Change to M.
2nd rib row P1, [k1, p1] to end.
With M, rep the last 2 rows twice more.
Change to size 3 needles.
Beg with a k row, work in St st and stripes of 2 rows C and 2 rows M, until back measures 5$\frac{1}{2}$ (6: 6$\frac{1}{4}$: 7$\frac{1}{2}$: 8$\frac{3}{4}$)in from cast-on edge, ending with a p row.
Shape armholes
Keeping St st stripes correct as set throughout, bind off 3 (3: 3: 4: 4) sts at beg of next 2 rows.
Next row K2, skp, k to last 4 sts, k2tog, k2.
Next row P to end.
Rep the last 2 rows 3 (4: 5: 5: 6) times. 51 (55: 59: 63: 67) sts.
Work even until back measures 9$\frac{1}{2}$ (10$\frac{1}{4}$: 11: 12$\frac{1}{2}$: 14$\frac{1}{4}$)in from cast-on edge, ending with a p row.
Shape shoulders
Bind off 12 (13: 14: 15: 16) sts at beg of next 2 rows.
Leave rem 27 (29: 31: 33: 35) sts on a holder.

left front

With size 2 needles and C, cast on 33 (35: 39: 41: 45) sts.
1st rib row P1, [k1, p1] to end.
Change to M.
2nd rib row K1, [p1, k1] to end.
With M, rep the last 2 rows twice more.
Change to size 3 needles.**
Beg with a k row, work in St st and stripes of 2 rows C and 2 rows M until front measures 5$\frac{1}{2}$ (6: 6$\frac{1}{4}$: 7$\frac{1}{2}$: 8$\frac{3}{4}$)in from cast-on edge, ending with the same stripe row as Back.
Shape armhole
Keeping St st stripes correct as set throughout, bind off 3 (3: 3: 4: 4) sts at beg of next row.
Work 1 row.
Next row K2, skp, k to end.
Next row P to end.
Rep the last 2 rows 3 (4: 5: 5: 6) times. 26 (27: 30: 31: 34) sts.
Work even until front measures 7$\frac{1}{2}$ (8$\frac{1}{4}$: 8$\frac{3}{4}$: 10$\frac{1}{4}$: 11$\frac{1}{2}$)in from cast-on edge, ending with a p row.
Shape neck
Next row K to last 4 (5: 5: 5: 6) sts and leave these sts on a holder.
Dec 1 st at neck edge on every row until 12 (13: 14: 15: 16) sts rem.
Work even until front measures same as Back to shoulder, ending at armhole edge.
Shape shoulder
Bind off.

right front

Work as given for Left Front to **.
Beg with a k row, cont in St st and stripes of 2 rows C and 2 rows M until front measures
5$^1/_2$ (6: 6$^1/_4$: 7$^1/_2$: 8$^3/_4$)in from cast-on edge, working one more row than on Left Front.
Shape armhole
Keeping St st stripes correct as set throughout, bind off 3 (3: 3: 4: 4) sts at beg of next row.
Next row K to last 4 sts, k2tog, k2.
Next row P to end.
Rep the last 2 rows 3 (4: 5: 5: 6) times. 26 (27: 30: 31: 34) sts.
Work even until front measures 7$^1/_2$ (8$^1/_4$: 8$^3/_4$: 10$^1/_4$: 11$^1/_2$)in from cast-on edge, ending with a p row.
Shape neck
Next row K4 (5: 5: 5: 6) sts, leave these sts on a holder, k to end.
Dec 1 st at neck edge on every row until 12 (13: 14: 15: 16) sts rem.
Work even until front measures same as Back to shoulder, ending at armhole edge.
Shape shoulder
Bind off.

sleeves

With size 2 needles and C, cast on 34 (36: 38: 40: 42) sts.
1st rib row [K1, p1] to end.
Change to M.
With M, rep the last row 5 times more.
Change to size 3 needles.
Beg with a k row, work in St st and stripes of 2 rows C and 2 rows M and **at the same time** inc
1 st at each end of the 3rd row and every foll 4th row until there are 54 (56: 60: 68: 74) sts.
Working in St st stripes as set throughout, work even until sleeve measures 6 (6$^3/_4$: 7$^1/_2$: 8$^1/_2$:
9$^1/_2$)in from cast-on edge, ending with the same stripe row as on Back to armhole.
Shape sleeve cap
Bind off 3 (3: 3: 4: 4) sts at beg of next 2 rows.
Next row K2, skp, k to last 4 sts, k2tog, k2.
Next row P to end.
Rep the last 2 rows 3 (4: 5: 5: 6) times. 40 (40: 42: 48: 52) sts.
Bind off.

neckband

Sew shoulder seams.
With right side facing, size 2 needles, and M, slip 4 (5: 5: 5: 6) sts on right front holder onto a
needle, pick up and k 17 (17: 18: 19: 19) sts up right front neck, k 27 (29: 31: 33: 35) sts from back
neck holder, pick up and k 17 (17: 18: 19: 19) sts down left front neck, then k 4 (5: 5: 5: 6) sts
from left front holder. 69 (73: 77: 81: 85) sts.
1st row P1, [k1, p1] to end.
2nd row K1, [p1, k1] to end.
These 2 rows form the rib.
Work 3 rows more in rib.
Change to C.
Rib 1 row.
Bind off in rib.

button band	With right side facing, size 2 needles, and M, pick up and k 55 (61: 63: 71: 77) sts along left front edge.

With right side facing, size 2 needles, and M, pick up and k 55 (61: 63: 71: 77) sts along left front edge.
Work 5 rows in rib as given for Neckband.
Change to C.
Rib 1 row.
Bind off in rib.

buttonhole band

With right side facing, size 2 needles and M, pick up and k 55 (61: 63: 71: 77) sts along right front edge.
Work 2 rows in rib as given for Neckband.
Buttonhole row Rib 1 (2: 3: 1: 1), [rib 2tog, yo, rib 8 (9: 9: 9: 10) sts] 5 (5: 5: 6: 6) times, rib 2tog, yo, rib 2 (2: 3: 2: 2).
Rib 2 rows.
Change to C.
Rib 1 row.
Bind off in rib.

to finish

Sew sleeves into armholes, matching stripes on shaping and easing in bound-off edge to fit.
Sew side and sleeve seams. Sew on buttons.

size
To fit ages 3–6 months

materials
1 x 1³/₄oz/50g ball Debbie Bliss Baby Cashmerino in each of gray (M) and ecru (C)
Pair of size 2 knitting needles

gauge
28 sts and 37 rows to 4in square over St st using size 2 needles.

abbreviations
See page 25.

striped booties

to make

With size 2 needles and M, cast on 36 sts and k 1 row.
1st row (right side) K1, yo, k16, yo, [k1, yo] twice, k16, yo, k1.
2nd and all wrong side rows K to end, working k1 tbl into each yo of previous row.
3rd row K2, yo, k16, yo, k2, yo, k3, yo, k16, yo, k2.
5th row K3, yo, k16, yo, [k4, yo] twice, k16, yo, k3.
7th row K4, yo, k16, yo, k5, yo, k6, yo, k16, yo, k4.
9th row K5, yo, k16, yo, [k7, yo] twice, k16, yo, k5.
11th row K22, yo, k8, yo, k9, yo, k22. 64 sts.
12th row Rep 2nd row.
Beg with a k row, cont in St st stripes of 2 rows C, 2 rows M throughout as follows:
Work 10 rows.
Shape instep
Next row K36, skp, turn.
Next row Sl 1, p8, p2tog, turn.
Next row Sl 1, k8, skp, turn.
Rep the last 2 rows 7 times more, then work first of the 2 rows again.
Next row Sl 1, k to end.
Next row P17, p2tog, p8, p2tog tbl, p17. 44 sts.
Break off C and cont in M only.
Next row [K1, p1] to end.
Rep the last row 11 times more.
Change to C.
Rib 1 row and bind off in rib.

to finish

Sew sole and back seam.

building blocks

measurements
Each block measures approximately 3in x 3in x 3in

materials
1 x 1³/₄oz/50g ball Debbie Bliss Baby Cashmerino in each of indigo (A), duck egg (B), lime (C), raspberry (D), silver (E), and camel (F)
Small amount of brown yarn for embroidery
Pair of size 2 knitting needles
5 foam blocks, each 3in x 3in x 3in

gauge
26 sts and 36 rows over St st to 4in square using size 2 needles.

abbreviations
See page 25.

note
Each of the five blocks of the building blocks set is made from six different knitted faces.

plain face
(make 5)

With size 2 needles and A, cast on 19 sts.
Seed st row K1, [p1, k1] to end.
Rep the seed st row 31 times more.
Bind off in seed st.
Make 4 more plain faces in same way, working one in each of B, C, D, and E.

narrow stripe face
(make 5)

With size 2 needles and A, cast on 19 sts.
Work in garter st stripe sequence as follows:
*K 1 row A, 2 rows B, 2 rows C, 2 rows D, 2 rows E, 2 rows F, 1 row A; rep from * twice more,
then k 1 row A, 2 rows B, 2 rows C, 1 row D.
Bind off knitwise in D.
Make 4 more narrow stripe faces in same way.

wide stripe face
(make 5)

With size 2 needles and A, cast on 19 sts.
Beg with a k row, work 27 rows in St st in stripe sequence as follows:
3 rows A, 1 row B, 1 row A, 3 rows B, 1 row C, 1 row B, 3 rows C, 1 row D, 1 row C, 3 rows D,
1 row E, 1 row D, 3 rows E, 1 row F, 1 row E, 2 rows F.
Bind off knitwise in F.
Make 4 more wide stripe faces in same way.

bear face
(make 5)

With size 2 needles and E, cast on 19 sts.
Beg with a k row, work 28 rows in St st from bear chart on page 140, using E for background and
F for bear.
Bind off purlwise.
Embroider eyes, snout, and mouth with brown yarn.
Make 4 more bear faces in same way, using F for all the bears and A or E for background.

bird's-eye spot face
(make 5)

With size 2 needles and background color of your choice, cast on 19 sts.
Beg with a k row, work 28 rows in St st from bird's-eye spot chart using spot color of your choice.
Bind off.
Make 4 more bird's-eye spot faces in same way, using a different color combination for each one.

number face
(make 5)

With size 2 needles and background color of your choice, cast on 19 sts.
Beg with a k row, work 28 rows in St st from number chart "1" using number color of your choice.
Bind off.
Make 4 more number faces in same way, using a different number (2, 3, 4, and 5) and a different
color combination for each one.

to finish

For each of the five blocks, select one of each of the six different faces and sew them together
as follows:
Sew four faces together in a strip; then sew the remaining two faces to the strip as shown in the
assembly diagram on page 140. Sew the first face to the fourth face of the strip of four, then sew
the remaining three sides of one of the side faces to the other faces. Insert the foam block and
sew the remaining three sides to the other faces.

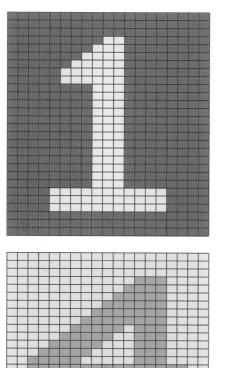

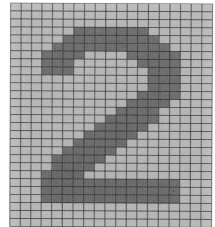

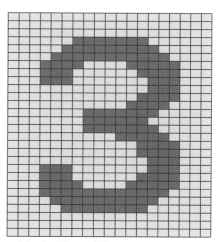

each face has 19 sts and 28 rows

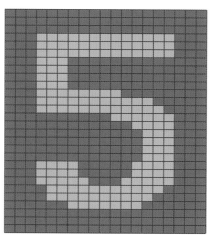

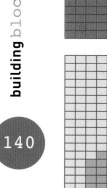

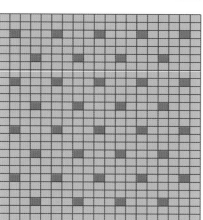

assembly diagram

yarn distributors

For stockists of Debbie Bliss yarns please contact:

USA
Knitting Fever Inc.
315 Bayview Avenue
Amityville
NY 11701
USA
t: +1 516 546 3600
f: +1 516 546 6871
w: www.knittingfever.com

CANADA
Diamond Yarns Ltd.
155 Martin Ross Avenue Unit 3
Toronto
Ontario M3J 2L9
Canada
t: +1 416 736 6111
f: +1 416 736 6112
w: www.diamondyarn.com

UK & WORLDWIDE DISTRIBUTORS
Designer Yarns Ltd.
Units 8–10
Newbridge Industrial Estate
Pitt Street, Keighley
W. Yorkshire BD21 4PQ, UK
t: +44 (0) 1535 664222
f: +44 (0) 1535 664333
e: alex@designeryarns.uk.com
w: www.designeryarns.uk.com

MEXICO
Estambres Crochet SA de CV
Aaron Saenz 1891-7
Col. Santa Maria, Monterrey
N.L. 64650, Mexico
t: +52 (81) 8335 3870
e: abremer@redmundial.com.mx

BELGIUM/HOLLAND
Pavan
Thomas Van Theemsche
Meerlaanstraat 73
9860 Balegem (Oostrezele)
Belgium
t: +32 (0) 9 221 85 94
f: +32 (0) 9 221 56 62
e: pavan@pandora.be

DENMARK
Fancy Knit
Hovedvejen 71
8586 Oerum Djurs
Ramten, Denmark
t: +45 59 46 21 89
f: +45 59 46 8018
e: roenneburg@mail.dk

FINLAND
Priima Käsityötalo
Hämeentie 26
00530 Helsinki, Finland
t: +358 9 7318 0010
f: +358 9 7318 0009
e: info@priima.net
w: www.priima.fi

FRANCE
Laines Plassard
La Filature
71800 Varennes-sous-Dun
France
w: www.laines-plassard.com

**GERMANY/AUSTRIA/
SWITZERLAND/LUXEMBOURG**
Designer Yarns (Deutschland)
GmbH
Sachsstraße 30
D-50259 Pulheim-Brauweiler
Germany
t: +49 (0) 2234 205453
f: +49 (0) 2234 205456
e: info@designeryarns.de
w: www.designeryarns.de

ICELAND
Storkurinn ehf
Laugavegi 59
101 Reykjavík, Iceland
t: +354 551 8258
f: +354 562 8252
e: storkurinn@simnet.is

SPAIN
Oyambre Needlework SL
Balmes, 200 At. 4
08006 Barcelona, Spain
t: +34 (0) 93 487 26 72
f: +34 (0) 93 218 66 94
e: info@oyambreonline.com

SWEDEN
Nysta garn och textil
Hogasvagen 20
S-131 47 Nacka, Sweden
t: +46 (0) 8 612 0330
e: info@nysta.se
w: www.nysta.se

RUSSIA
Taiga Publishing
ul. Srednaja Pervomajskaja 4/1
Moscow Russian Federation
105077
Russia
t: +7 (495) 786 8274
e: info@debbiebliss.ru

AUSTRALIA/NEW ZEALAND
Prestige Yarns Pty Ltd
PO Box 39
Bulli
NSW 2516, Australia
t: +61 (0) 2 4285 6669
e: info@prestigeyarns.com
w: www.prestigeyarns.com

TAIWAN
U-Knit
1F, 199-1 Sec
Zhong Xiao East Road
Taipei, Taiwan
t: +886 2 27527557
f: +886 2 27528556
e: shuindigo@hotmail.com

BRAZIL
Quatro Estacoes Com
Las Linhas e Acessorios Ltda
Av. Das Nacoes Unidas
12551-9 Andar
Cep 04578-000 Sao Paulo
Brazil
t: +55 11 3443 7736
e: cristina@4estacoeslas.com.br

For more information on my other books and yarns, please visit www.debbieblissonline.com

First published in the United States of America in 2009 by **Trafalgar Square Books** North Pomfret, Vermont 05053

Printed in China

Originally published in the United Kingdom in 2009 by Quadrille Publishing Limited, London.

Text and project designs
© 2009 Debbie Bliss
Photography, design, and layout
© 2009 Quadrille Publishing Limited

Editorial Director **Jane O'Shea**
Creative Director **Mary Evans**
Project Editor **Lisa Pendreigh**
Photographer **Ulla Nyeman**
Stylist **Julie Mansfield**
Illustrator **Kate Simunek**
Pattern Illustrator **Bridget Bodoano**
Production Director **Vincent Smith**
Production Controller **Ruth Deary**

ISBN: 978-1-57076-438-7

Library of Congress Control Number:
2009903524

10 9 8 7 6 5 4 3 2 1

First Edition

144

acknowledgments

This book wouldn't have been possible without the generous collaboration of the following:

Rosy Tucker, who produced all the wonderful toys, big and little birds, and the memory book. Her practical and creative input is always invaluable. Also for the pattern checking.

Penny Hill, for her essential pattern compiling.

Jane O'Shea, **Lisa Pendreigh**, and **Mary Evans** at Quadrille Publishing for being such a wonderful team to work with.

Julie Mansfield for the perfect styling and overall look.

Ulla Nyeman for the beautiful photography.

Jo Gillingwater for the great job baby grooming.

And, of course, the fantastic babies: **Alara, Anwyn, Conor, Daisy, Dotty, Frankie, Jago, Laud, Luca, Luna, Mimi, Monty, Reggie,** and **Robyn**.

The knitters, for the huge effort they put into creating perfect knits under deadline pressure: **Cynthia Brent, Barbara Clapham, Pat Church, Jacqui Dunt, Shirley Kennet, Maisie Lawrence,** and **Frances Wallace**.

My fantastic agent, **Heather Jeeves.**

The distributors, agents, retailers, and **knitters** who support all my books and yarns with such enthusiasm and make what I do possible.